Contents

Introduction

Teaching and learning subjects via cross-curricular routes is complicated – and coordination of how Citizenship can be taught *through* other subjects can be complex. Teachers have not been overwhelmed with advice and resources in this area (the best guide is *Making Sense of Citizenship: A Continuing Professional Development Handbook*, Eds. Ted Huddleston & David Kerr, Chapter 4 [Hodder Murray/Citizenship Foundation, 2006]). Inspection evidence has accumulated that cross-curricular approaches to Citizenship are often lacking in terms of both definition and rigour. For example, an OFSTED annual subject report noted: 'Where schools have chosen a cross-curricular approach in which the citizenship elements are implicit, there is no tangible programme overall, and pupils are not necessarily aware that they are studying Citizenship' (OFSTED, 2003). This series aims to help all secondary teachers make exciting and engaging connections between their specialist subjects and Citizenship, and to help Citizenship education coordinators find willing allies all around their school.

For contributions from other subjects to be officially classified as part of the Citizenship curriculum, simply identifying common concerns and a coincidence of content is not enough. Lessons should have a specific Citizenship orientation – in terms of concepts, skills, participation, and advocacy as well as knowledge content. Citizenship education at its heart involves students' engaging in some kind of a 'change action'. Having learnt about and researched an issue, they then seek to do something about it and 'make a difference'. The change action does not necessarily mean changing the world, but working towards something that aims to communicate knowledge and understanding to others in a persuasive way – for example, the creation of a display, a PowerPoint® presentation, a role play or an assembly designed for peers or younger students – in other words, conscious acts of advocacy directed at an internal or external audience which aim to engage hearts and minds. It is about young people being able to imagine a better local and global future and having the knowledge, skills and self-confidence to take some practical steps to achieving that future. All of the contributors to this series share this underpinning philosophy.

All of the texts in this series clearly cross-reference the links between individual subject learning outcomes and Citizenship learning outcomes against the latest National Curriculum Programmes of Study. Each book contains five units of work (themes) each with four or five lesson ideas and resources. Key questions for the lessons provide focus and direction. We also offer a range of possible assessment activities through the units of work which support both 'assessment for learning' teaching approaches and summative 'assessment of learning' opportunities.

Assessing the Citizenship curriculum has proved difficult for teachers. There can be a lack of clarity in relation to who is responsible for assessing students' Citizenship work across the curriculum and there are few developed models and mechanisms for doing this effectively. Too often, cross-curricular approaches to Citizenship education begin and end with a curriculum audit with little subsequent exploration of the implications of ticking a particular box. Coherence and imaginative learning activities and teaching skills are required to truly bring the subject and Citizenship links to life and to stimulate deep student learning and engagement.

In this *Citizenship through informed and responsible action* contribution to the series, the authors focus particularly on the development of Citizenship skills and processes. The units of work explore the building blocks of active Citizenship through focusing upon identity (mantras and manifestos); individual change-makers; and the skills of advocacy and persuasion. Theme four investigates the role of the media in campaigning, whilst the final theme provides frameworks for planning and reviewing collaborative Citizenship action. Like all of the contributions to this series, they foreground controversial issues which aim to spark young people's interest and there are many opportunities to develop students' political literacy. The units are designed to be used flexibly across Years 7 to 11, depending upon students' interest and prior attainment, but the latter two units are likely to work better at Key Stage 4.

Peter Brett
Series Editor

Progression tool

Getting better at Citizenship: Providing a 'staircase' of progression from Year 7 to Year 11

Finding ways to assess students' learning in Citizenship has been a big challenge for Citizenship teachers. This is particularly so when we recognize the range of Citizenship cognitive and personal qualities that are being assessed; for example,

- **knowledge** about key values, processes (such as political decision-making) and concepts (such as democracy or justice and fairness)
- **skills** like enquiry (identifying issues of concern, researching evidence, reaching conclusions, proposing action), debate and communication (listening, talking, writing, expressing, persuading, and so on)
- **participation in and outside school** (teamwork, leadership, managing, supporting, recording and evaluating).

The challenges are extended when Citizenship is taught and assessed in cross-curricular contexts. Try to help your Citizenship coordinator to provide some coherence by making just two or three explicit and recorded contributions to the Citizenship assessment process through your subject context.

The new National Curriculum attainment target for the end of Key Stage 3 provides a guide of the standards to aim for. Level descriptions (an eight level scale plus exceptional performance) seek to provide clear standards for achievement for Key Stage 3 and beyond. The QCA argue that the purpose of the move towards an eight level scale for Citizenship is to improve the performance of students in Citizenship and also improve teacher understanding about standards in Citizenship, leading to more consistency in teacher judgement based on a wider range of evidence. It also enables a parity of status with other Key Stage 3 foundation subjects.

There is a statutory requirement for teachers to assess student attainment in Citizenship at the end of Key Stage 3. From the summer of 2011 this assessment must be carried out using the level descriptions, with teachers needing to decide which level description best fits each student's attainment based on the evidence they have. They must also continue to provide a written annual report to parents on strengths and areas for development in Citizenship for each student in Years 7 to 11.

This may sound like an assessment juggernaut, crushing creativity beneath its bureaucratic embrace, but the mindmap below sets out to indicate how the process of assessing progress in Citizenship can be meaningful and manageable.

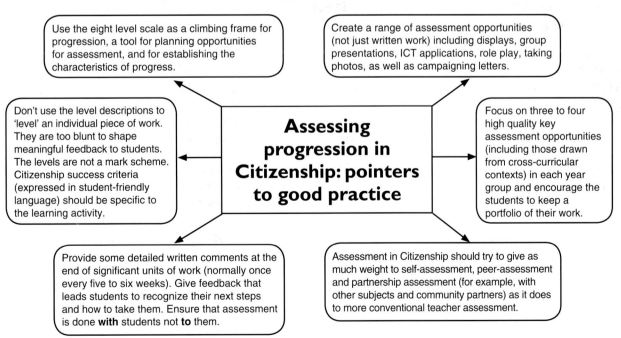

The success criteria levelling grid on the next page is generic ... and one key principle of success criteria for the range of Citizenship activities contained in this series is that they need to be task-specific. However, this framework of progression should be adaptable to different units of work and the 'big' half-termly planned assessment activities.

Success Criteria Levelling Grid for students

The squares show how you can build your achievement from the top row (Level 3) down to the bottom row (Level 8+). If you can show that you are able to do all of the tasks in the squares along the row well, you can award yourself or your partner that level. Your teacher will then let you know if they agree.

Knowledge/critical thinking	Enquiry/research/ questioning	Working with others/ speaking out	Taking action	Self Level	Teacher Level
I recognize that issues affect people in my neighbourhood and community in different ways. I have a simple understanding of political issues as far as they impact on my own life.	I can find information from more than one source provided for me.	I am starting to work constructively with other students on Citizenship enquiries. I can present to others and begin to acknowledge different responses to my ideas.	I know that people have a say in what happens locally and nationally. I take part in decision-making activities with others on Citizenship issues.	3	3
I can show some factual knowledge and understanding of Citizenship issues that I have explored and a basic understanding of some Citizenship concepts.	I have used a range of information, including ICT and the media, to find out about a Citizenship topic. I am starting to ask questions to explore issues and problems.	I make contributions to class debates. I have used my understanding to make a presentation on a Citizenship issue. I can work together with others to plan a course of action.	I have suggested some things that people can do to change things for the better.	4	4
As 4, but I am showing a broader understanding of Citizenship issues and concepts and starting to make links between key events and ideas. I can show some knowledge of the operation of the political and justice systems in the UK.	As 4, plus I can explain why I select sources. I have used different methods of enquiry and sources of information to investigate issues.	As 4, plus I have considered a range of views and drawn my own conclusions about what can be done. I can be an active member of a group, making a positive contribution to team tasks.	As 4, plus I can work with others, to negotiate, plan and carry out actions aimed at making a difference to the lives of others and can start to explain the impact of actions taken.	5	5
As 5, plus I can develop informed arguments, taking account of diverse viewpoints. I can discuss a range of political issues in some depth including starting to engage with abstract ideas.	As 5, plus I am using information critically to reach conclusions. I use a wide range of research strategies and sources of information to help to put together my presentation/piece of work.	As 5, plus I can present a persuasive case for a particular course of action, giving reasons for my view. I show respect for other people's values and commitments.	As 5, but additionally I demonstrate a deep understanding of how individuals can make a difference to society.	6	6
As 6, plus I have a detailed understanding of the key Citizenship concepts of democracy, justice, rights and responsibilities, identities and diversity, including how these can change over time.	As 6, plus I am demonstrating initiative in my research. I can interpret different sources of information and am alert to assessing these for validity and bias.	As 6, plus I often take a lead in group and decision-making activities. I demonstrate increasing self-awareness about my own assumptions and views.	As 6, plus I am able to explain how the actions of individuals and groups can affect the behaviour of governments.	7	7
As 7, plus I can use and apply sophisticated knowledge of Citizenship issues, problems and events to analyse how these affect groups and communities in different parts of the world.	As 7, plus I can independently create other lines of enquiry.	As 7, plus I demonstrate a nuanced sense of empathy, using an informed imagination to consider the views and experiences of others.	As 7, plus I take a leading role in defining, negotiating, undertaking and evaluating courses of action with others to address Citizenship issues and problems.	8+	8+

Curriculum links

Citizenship

1 Key concepts for KS3 and KS4

	1.1 Democracy and justice				1.2 Rights and responsibilities			1.3 Identities and diversity: living together in the UK			
	a	b	c	d	a	b	c	a	b	c	d
Theme 1	✓	✓			✓			✓		✓	✓
Theme 2	✓	✓	✓	✓	✓		✓	✓			✓
Theme 3				✓	✓	✓				✓	
Theme 4					✓					✓	✓
Theme 5	✓	✓	✓	✓	✓	✓	✓	✓	✓	✓	✓

2 Key processes for KS3

	2.1 Critical thinking and enquiry			2.2 Advocacy and representation				2.3 Taking informed and responsible action			
	a	b	c	a	b	c	d	a	b	c	d
Theme 1	✓			✓	✓	✓	✓	✓	✓	✓	✓
Theme 2	✓			✓	✓	✓	✓	✓	✓	✓	✓
Theme 3	✓	✓	✓	✓	✓	✓	✓	✓	✓	✓	✓

2 Key processes for KS4

	2.1 Critical thinking and enquiry				2.2 Advocacy and representation			2.3 Taking informed and responsible action				
	a	b	c	d	a	b	c	a	b	c	d	e
Theme 4	✓		✓	✓	✓	✓	✓	✓	✓	✓		✓
Theme 5	✓	✓	✓	✓	✓	✓	✓	✓	✓	✓	✓	✓

3 Range and content for KS3

	a	b	c	d	e	f	g	h	i	j	k
Theme 1				✓	✓	✓					
Theme 2	✓	✓		✓	✓				✓		
Theme 3				✓	✓						

3 Range and content for KS4

	a	b	c	d	e	f	g	h	i	j	k	l	m	n
Theme 4							✓							
Theme 5							✓	✓						

4 Curriculum opportunities for KS3

	a	b	c	d	e	f	g	h	i	j
Theme 1	✓	✓	✓		✓		✓	✓	✓	
Theme 2	✓	✓	✓				✓	✓	✓	
Theme 3	✓	✓	✓		✓		✓	✓	✓	✓

4 Curriculum opportunities for KS4

	a	b	c	d	e	f	g	h	i	j
Theme 4	✓	✓	✓				✓	✓	✓	✓
Theme 5	✓	✓	✓	✓	✓	✓	✓	✓	✓	✓

Theme one
Values and voice – exploring my identity

The opening theme focuses on student voice. The lessons are designed for young people to analyse their own belief systems and those of their peers. The activities provide a basis for some of the challenges in later themes which require the students to debate and justify their viewpoints publicly, to find an issue they feel passionately about, and to take action.

We hope that the resources challenge young people to think about their individual views and also their collective thoughts as a class. This will lay the foundations for self-motivation and confident class communication. The quieter members of the group may need support in being able to share their opinions. Some of the activities contained within this theme will allow the more expressive students a chance to lead others; this must be closely monitored to ensure that the class viewpoints are a real representation of all students and not just the persuasive minority!

There are opportunities later in the theme for class debates around a number of controversial issues, so it is important to adjust suggested topics to suit the particular sensitivities of the group.

Theme aims:

- To enable students to gain understanding of their individual viewpoints on a number of controversial issues.

- To support students in developing appropriate means of self-expression.

- To give students the confidence to challenge the opinions of others appropriately.

Lesson One: Mantras

Learning objectives:

- To recognize a mantra, and how it is used to motivate individuals to action
- To understand what motivates us as individuals to succeed, recognizing that different people have different aims
- To set targets for areas of our own lives that we want to improve.

Resources: 1.1, 1.2, 1.3

Starter:
Ask the students to describe what they think a 'mantra' is, using the points below for guidance. Sharing your own personal mantra is good way to get the discussion going.

A mantra …

- is a personal statement repeated over and over that inspires you to success and helps you to remain focused on a goal
- reminds you of what you believe in and what motivates you to achieve.

A mantra must be: personal to you, short (no more than two sentences), high-reaching, repeated over and over, positive.

Main activity:
Read the mantras on Resource 1.1 aloud with the class. After each one, ask the class to explain the mantra, using modern and relevant examples wherever possible, to illustrate the meaning and intention.

Before the lesson you will need to make copies of the table on Resource 1.2 and cut the mantras and information about people into separate pieces of paper; mix the pieces of paper up before giving them to groups of students. Working in pairs or threes, ask students to match the mantras to the people who said them using the information about their achievements to help.

Having worked through this task, ask students to think about which mantras appeal to them directly. Working individually, students choose three mantras they like, and write these and the reasons why they like them in their books. Ask students to choose one mantra that they could apply to their own life, and then write and decorate it in their journal/planner.

Working individually, students now write their own unique personal mantra using Resource 1.3 as a guide. Read through the resource together as a class.

Plenary:
If they are comfortable to do so, ask students to share areas of their lives they want to improve.

Assessment/Extension activity:
Students should hand write their new, personal mantra created using Resource 1.3 on a piece of card and put it somewhere they will see it often, for example on their desk, by their computer or attached to a bedroom mirror.

Lesson Two: Manifestos

Learning objectives:

- To recognize a manifesto, understand how it is used, and by whom
- To produce a class manifesto, created through both individual and collective decision making, that will underpin all subsequent Citizenship classes
- To understand that action comes out of democracy but that not everyone will get their own way in the democratic process.

Resources: 1.4, 1.5, 1.6, 1.7

Starter:
Ask students, 'What is a manifesto?' Encourage them to create their own definition, using the following points for inspiration.

A manifesto:

- is a public document
- states the purpose, principles or plan of action of a group or individual
- contains a set number of points, statements of intent or pledges
- helps gather other people's support
- aims to create social change
- sets out an agreed agenda.

Ask students to think about which groups or individuals might use a manifesto.

Main activity:
Students look at a selection of manifestos on Resources 1.4 and 1.5. You might want to read out the background information to each example before students, in pairs, read through the manifestos. As they are reading, encourage students to think about why each manifesto is effective and why it has been used. When they have read the examples, ask them to feed back why they think the group or individual has used a manifesto in each instance. Here are some suggestions.

Because they:

- are a clear way of presenting important information
- are precise and to the point

- are easy for a wide range of people to understand
- sum up the intentions of a group or party
- encourage public support
- have powerful historical and political associations with creating social change.

It is not an original idea to have a document on the wall, instructing students as to the rules of that particular classroom. A class manifesto is slightly different though, as the majority group (the young people) will be deciding the rules in the best interests of everyone. As a class, create a manifesto to guide all Citizenship lessons from now on. In order for the manifesto to work effectively, everyone (including you) must broadly support its aims. However, it is unlikely that *everyone* will support *all* points. Where students disagree on a point they must debate until a satisfactory conclusion is reached. This is a good point to lead into a discussion about democracy, the role of negotiation and persuasion, and to develop an understanding that in a democratic process not everyone gets what they want.

Start by asking students to spend ten minutes completing Step 1 on Resource 1.6, to think of three things that would make their Citizenship classes better. When they have completed this task encourage them to spend another ten minutes completing Step 2 in small groups, comparing their ideas and writing down those that others agree with. This helps to give an idea of which ideas are the strongest and most likely to make it onto the manifesto.

Next, ask students to spend ten minutes writing down their own ideas for the class manifesto, listing five points. Then, in groups of about eight, students must decide on eight ideas that they all agree on to take back to the class. The group should nominate one person to write up the final ideas and report back.

Plenary:
Bring the whole class back together and ask each group to feed back their points, writing all of them on the board. The class now needs to decide on the eight points which make the final manifesto, with the class voting on *every* idea. Count the number of votes for each manifesto point, and the eight points with the highest number of votes make it onto the final document (Resource 1.7).

At the end of the lesson, type up the final list, enlarge and copy it for the next lesson, to be displayed prominently around the classroom. This is important to demonstrate that action comes out of democracy!

Lesson Three: Moral dilemmas

Learning objectives:
- To use reasoning, discussion and debating skills to formulate a response to a complex social/moral problem which has no clear right or wrong answer
- To create an original moral dilemma.

Resources: 1.8, 1.9, 1.10

Starter:
The classroom needs to be rearranged prior to the start of this lesson. The students must be sat informally in clusters of five. Try to avoid tables within the clusters as the aim is for students to feel removed from a standard teaching environment. This lesson works best with a class atmosphere of informality and where students feel relaxed.

Split the class into groups of five students, allocating one person in each group as timekeeper. Give each student one of the scenarios on Resource 1.8 and ask them to read it.

Main activity:
Working in their groups, students take it in turns to read out the moral dilemma on their card, challenging the others to say what they would do in that situation and to discuss their reasoning. They must discuss every dilemma and challenge each other when they believe the solutions provided are not appropriate or well thought out. Spend five minutes on each card. Ask students to write down their group's solutions, including reasons this solution would/wouldn't work as discussed by the group.

Citizenship through informed and responsible action   © Folens (copiable page)

Now ask each group to write its own original moral dilemma scenario (Resource 1.9). This should be an issue the group would find it difficult to solve, where there is no clear-cut answer. Ask students to make sure the dilemma is not personal and doesn't relate to someone who is in the class. Ask groups to swap their new dilemmas and suggest solutions.

Plenary:
Conduct a whole-class discussion regarding the dilemmas and the suggested actions. Encourage the class to challenge each other and to debate answers that they feel are immoral, impractical or unworkable.

Then collect the examples of students' own moral dilemmas – these are a valuable resource for future lessons and for different teaching groups.

Extension activity:
Give each student one of the extended narrative moral dilemmas on Resource 1.10 or 1.11. Ask them to write a one-page response about what should be done in that situation. You can then analyse and discuss the responses in the next lesson with the whole class.

Lesson Four: My standpoint

Learning objectives:
- To identify individual viewpoints on a number of topical controversial issues and to recognize that others may disagree
- To form arguments and convince others of different viewpoints.

Resource: 1.12

Starter:
Explain that this lesson will be about students identifying their own standpoints on a number of controversial issues, about which there are no right or wrong answers. Make it clear at the start of the session that this lesson will be about exploring personal boundaries and that people should feel free to be honest about their opinions. However, they must be sensitive to other people's feelings and must be aware of respecting other's opinions, even when their viewpoints are opposed in some way.

Main activity:
Work through the following controversial issues, playing the Yes/No game:

1. Teachers should be allowed to use physical restraint on students.
2. Animal testing for medical research is appropriate.
3. Women should be allowed to fight on the front line in the army.
4. Cannabis should be decriminalized.
5. It should be made illegal for pregnant women to smoke cigarettes.
6. The death sentence should be applied to child killers in this country.
7. The age of sexual consent should be raised to 18 to help prevent teenage pregnancy and the spread of STIs.
8. Schools should be free of all religious teaching.
9. A teacher should be free to form relationships with sixth-formers if consensual.
10. British politics interests me.
11. All convicted paedophiles should be chemically castrated.
12. Immigration in Britain should be stopped or drastically cut.
13. The British class system still exists.
14. I am confident about my looks and my body image.
15. Barack Obama's election proves that America is a less racist society than Britain.
16. Knowing a high-street store used sweatshop labour, I would still shop there if the clothes were really cheap.
17. Selective schooling in Britain is unfair and leads to educational inequality.

This activity works best when there is plenty of space. This could be a good lesson to relocate to a drama space or to a school hall. Failing that, clear away all chairs and tables to enable the maximum amount of space for the activity.

Mark one side of the room with 'YES' and the other side of the room with 'NO'. There is no marking in the middle of the room and with this game there is no room for 'MAYBE'.

Take a prominent position at the front of the class and call out the questions, to which the students must decide if the answer is 'YES' (I agree with that statement) or 'NO' (I don't agree with that statement). Once they have decided the students should vote with their feet and stand on the corresponding side of the room. Make it clear that they must not just follow the majority crowd. After each question, choose one person randomly from YES to explain why they went and stood there and choose another person from NO to do the same. As the game progresses and the students grow in confidence, they will start challenging each other on the issues and their own personal standpoint and need less teacher intervention.

Reorganize the room, and move on to the next part of the lesson which will involve students using Resource 1.12 and debating a controversial issue. Divide the class in two. Ensure that the groups are equally weighted between higher-attaining, average-attaining and lower-attaining students. Choose a subject for the class to debate, using the list below for inspiration:

1. Politics is relevant to young people (KS3).
2. Schools are in touch with modern life (KS3).
3. Young people are demonized in modern society (KS4).
4. Personal relationships between teachers and students are immoral (KS4).

One group will argue 'FOR' the case and one group 'AGAINST'. Each group must decide on a group leader and has five minutes to prepare for 'battle'. The groups have to work together quickly to ensure that each member of the group knows what to say and feels equipped with a pertinent point of view. This is the opportunity for the 'leaders' to support their group and ensure that everyone feels able to contribute. It is a team debate so it is important that the higher-attaining members of the group spend time building the confidence of those who may struggle with the task.

Mark two spaces opposite each other on the floor and instruct speakers to stand on these to make their points. The two 'leaders' stand face to face with the rest of the class divided behind them, and each leader is allowed to make one point. The group arguing 'FOR' the statement should speak first and make their opening argument. The team arguing 'AGAINST' must respond and then they can make a point of their own. Ideally the activity will continue with a response and new point at each turn, and each member of the class will take a turn to step up and speak. No one can speak more than twice, so the group leaders cannot dominate and must encourage all members of their group to be involved. The game should flow very quickly and teams will be penalized if no one from their group steps forward to argue against a point developed by the opposing team. The team that wins is the one in which the most members have spoken and have been convincing in their arguments. Cooperation should be rewarded over individual brilliance and articulacy.

Plenary:
Ask the students to consider the following questions: Did anything surprise you in this lesson? Did any individual particularly impress you? Did you like or dislike so much talking/debating in the lesson? Is there enough opportunity to voice your opinions during time at school?

Resource 1.1: Mantras throughout history

Read through the following mantras. For each example, think about what the mantra means, and why the person would have used it.

Mantras from famous people:	Ordinary people use mantras too:
"You must be the change you wish to see in the world." – Mahatma Gandhi	"Just because you can, doesn't mean you should."
"Less is more." – Robert Browning	"Courage is not always loud. Sometimes it is a quiet voice saying 'I will try again tomorrow'."
"I don't have to be what you want me to be. I'm free to be what I want." – Muhammad Ali	"Live every day as if it is your last."
"Never squander what to others are riches." – Buddhist Proverb	"I have the right to exist, just as I am, and live just the way I want to."
"Opportunity is missed by most people because it is dressed in overalls and looks like work." – Thomas Edison	"Yesterday I did, today I do, and tomorrow I will."
"To thine own self be true." – William Shakespeare's *Hamlet*, Act I, Scene 3	"Live long, laugh often, love much."
"Done is better than perfect." – Anne Mollegen Smith	"When you stand for nothing, you'll fall for anything."
"Adventure without risk is Disneyland." – Douglas Coupland	"Hope for the best; prepare for the worst."

Resource 1.2: Match the mantras to the people and their achievements

Mantra	Name of person and significance
"An eye for an eye only ends up making the whole world blind."	**Mahatma Gandhi** (2 October 1869–30 January 1948) was the leader of the Indian nationalist movement and is officially honoured in India as the 'Father of the Nation'. His birthday is commemorated there as a national holiday and as the International Day of Non-Violence.
"If you want others to be happy, practice compassion. If you want to be happy, practice compassion."	**The Dalai Lama**, the spiritual and political leader of the Tibetan people according to Tibetan Buddhism.
"If a man has not discovered something that he will die for, he isn't fit to live."	**Martin Luther King Jr.** (15 January 1929–4 April 1968) was an African American clergyman, activist and prominent leader of the American civil rights movement.
"You could be the world's best garbage man, the world's best model; it don't matter what you do if you're the best."	**Muhammad Ali** (born 17 January 1942) is a retired American boxer and former three-times World Heavyweight Champion. In 1999, Ali was crowned 'BBC Sports Personality of the Century'.
"If you don't like something, change it. If you can't change it, change your attitude. Don't complain."	**Maya Angelou** (born 4 April 1928) is an American poet, memoirist, actress and prominent civil rights activist. She is seen as one of life's great survivors.
"We cannot do great things on this Earth. We can only do small things with great love."	**Blessed Mother Teresa of Calcutta** (27 August 1910–5 September 1997) was a nun who for over 45 years ministered to the poor, sick, orphaned and dying.
"It's not whether you win or lose, its how many people remember you when you die."	**Jonathan Ross, OBE** (born 17 November 1960) is a presenter of radio and television. Ross has a cheekiness in his style of presenting, and has often been surrounded in controversy.
"Ask not what your country can do for you. Ask what you can do for your country."	**John F. Kennedy** (29 May 1917–22 November 1963) was a popular President of the United States of America serving from 1961 until his assassination in 1963.
"If you're walking down the right path and you're willing to keep walking, eventually you'll make progress."	**Barack Obama Jr.** (born 4 August 1961) is the first African American to be elected President of the United States of America.
"Only put off until tomorrow what you are willing to die having left undone."	**Pablo Picasso** (25 October 1881–8 April 1973) was an Andalusian–Spanish painter, draughtsman and sculptor. He is one of the most influential figures in twentieth-century art.

Citizenship through informed and responsible action

Resource 1.3: Write your own personal mantra

Creating a mantra is a private task because it should be unique to you. What guides and motivates someone else through their life may have no impact on you personally whatsoever. The first rule of writing a mantra is to be honest with yourself. To accept the use of a mantra, you must first believe that you *need* one to help you! In order to do this you need to accept that there are some areas in your life in which you need to challenge yourself a little more. Reasons could include:

- Wanting to build your confidence to enable you to speak out in public
- Wanting to organize yourself to get up on time in the mornings!
- Wanting to manage your temper effectively so you don't get into trouble
- Wanting to prevent yourself getting into situations over which you have no control
- Finding the strength to face up to someone who is dominating/bullying you.

Things you'll need:

- Pen and paper
- A piece of A5 card

Read through the list of personal mantras on Resource 1.2. Find one that particularly attracts you and then adapt it to suit your own personal circumstance.

Think first ... What do I want my mantra to DO for me?

> Think about your personal issue. For example, lack of motivation:
> "I tend to give up when things seem particularly difficult or if someone puts me down. I want to be stronger and more determined to succeed."

> Choose an appropriate mantra from the list on Resource 1.2. For example, Barack Obama's
> "If you're walking down the right path and you're willing to keep walking, eventually you'll make progress."

> Personalize your chosen mantra. For example,
> "Once I'm on the right road, STAY ON IT until I reach my destination."

> Now that you've created your own unique mantra, type or hand write it on a piece of card and put it somewhere you will see it often.
>
> Make several copies, one for your bedroom, one for your diary and another for your desk. Repeat it to yourself several times throughout the day, silently or aloud. Make it a habit; repeat it first thing in the morning, before you go to bed and any time you find yourself focusing on the negative things your mantra is helping you to change.
>
> Hand one copy of your chosen mantra in to your teacher. They will not show anyone else.

Resource 1.4: Manifesto examples 1

Ten Commandments

A list of ten religious and moral rules which feature prominently in Christianity and Judaism.

1. You shall have no other god to set against me.

2. You shall not make a carved image for yourself nor the likeness of anything in the heavens above, or on the earth below, or in the waters under the earth.

3. You shall not make wrong use of the name of the LORD your God.

4. Remember to keep the sabbath day holy.

5. Honour your father and your mother, that you may live long in the land which the LORD your God is giving you.

6. You shall not commit murder.

7. You shall not commit adultery.

8. You shall not steal.

9. You shall not give false evidence against your neighbour.

10. You shall not covet your neighbour's house;... nor anything that belongs to him.

The Communist Manifesto

Written by Karl Marx and Friedrich Engels in 1848, this is one of the most influential political texts ever written. The book sets out a course of action for a working-class revolution, eventually bringing about an end to private property and a classless and stateless society. The text can be summarized into the following ten points:

1. Abolition of property in land and application of all rents of land to public purposes.

2. A heavy progressive or graduated income tax.

3. Abolition of all right of inheritance.

4. Confiscation of the property of all emigrants and rebels.

5. Centralization of credit in the hands of the State, by means of a national bank with State capital and an exclusive monopoly.

6. Centralization of the means of communication and transport in the hands of the State.

7. Extension of factories and instruments of production owned by the State; the bringing into cultivation of wastelands, and the improvement of the soil generally in accordance with a common plan.

8. Equal liability of all to labour. Establishment of industrial armies, especially for agriculture.

9. Combination of agriculture with manufacturing industries; gradual abolition of the distinction between town and country, by a more equable distribution of the population over the country.

10. Free education for all children in public schools. Abolition of children's factory labour in its present form. Combination of education with industrial production.

Black Panther Party: The Ten Point Program

The Black Panther Party was an African American organization active in the United States of America from the mid-1960s into the 1980s. The organization was initially set up with the aim of protecting African American neighbourhoods from police brutality. It went on to establish a variety of community programmes to reduce poverty and improve health among communities which needed help. The group created a 'Ten Point Program', a document that called for 'Land, Bread, Housing, Education, Clothing, Justice and Peace'.

1. **We want freedom. We want power to determine the destiny of our black and oppressed communities.**

2. **We want full employment for our people.**

3. **We want an end to the robbery by the capitalists of our black and oppressed communities.**

4. **We want decent housing, fit for the shelter of human beings.**

5. **We want decent education for our people that exposes the true nature of this decadent American society. We want education that teaches us our true history and our role in the present-day society.**

6. **We want completely free health care for all black and oppressed people.**

7. **We want an immediate end to police brutality and murder of black people, other people of color, all oppressed people inside the United States.**

8. **We want an immediate end to all wars of aggression.**

9. **We want freedom for all black and oppressed people now held in US federal, state, county, city and military prisons and jails. We want trials by a jury of peers for all persons charged with so-called crimes under the laws of this country.**

10. **We want land, bread, housing, education, clothing, justice, peace and people's community control of modern technology.**

Conservative Party Manifesto 2005

Conservatives are currently the largest opposition party in the United Kingdom.

More police

Cleaner hospitals

Lower taxes

School discipline

Controlled immigration

Accountability

Resource 1.6: A Citizenship class manifesto

There may be issues that are unique to your particular class, which could be helped by a class manifesto. Manifestos should not be about individuals though. So it wouldn't be appropriate to say, "Darren can't walk in late" or "Miss Clarke mustn't lose it with the girls on the back row"! This is about collective actions for the betterment of the whole group, that will help with the educational process.

Step 1
Individually, write down three REASONABLE and SENSIBLE things that could make your Citizenship lessons even better.

Three things that would improve Citizenship classes:
1.
2.
3.

Step 2
Discuss your points with other people and see if you agree on three key areas.

Key points that we agree on:
1.
2.
3.

Step 3
Write down your own five ideas for the class manifesto.

Citizenship class manifesto: my ideas
1.
2.
3.
4.
5.

Step 4
Get into groups and decide between you on eight ideas to propose for the Citizenship class manifesto that you can all agree on. Nominate one person to write these ideas up and report back to the rest of the class.

Citizenship through informed and responsible action

Resource 1.7: Our Citizenship class manifesto

Citizenship class manifesto
1.
2.
3.
4.
5.
6.
7.
8.

Resource 1.8: Moral dilemmas

1. A close friend confides to you that he has committed a crime. While drinking heavily, he beat someone up quite badly in a fight. You are shocked, but promise never to tell. Discovering that an innocent person has been accused of the crime, you plead with your friend to give himself up. He refuses completely and reminds you of your promise.

   What do you do?

2. Akeim sits next to Josh, the toughest and hardest boy in Year 10. Akeim's parents are quite strict, but Josh is allowed as much personal freedom as he wants and gets involved in street fights and gang activity. Akeim befriends Josh and goes to his house after school. He finds out that Josh's bruises aren't from street fights, but are inflicted by Josh's own father. Josh will probably beat up Akeim if he says anything, but Akeim feels that Josh is being abused.

   What should Akeim do?

3. When Gemma's parents go away for the weekend, she's thrilled to be trusted to stay alone. But her friends want to use her house for a party. Gemma doesn't feel comfortable with this, but knows that this is what happens when parents are away and she has attended all the house parties of people in her class. In fact, she has been involved in pressurizing people into opening their homes for parties. Gemma's mum has made her promise that she won't let people into the house whilst they are away. Gemma has a close relationship with her mum and doesn't like to lie to her.

   What should Gemma do?

4. You are coming out of the train station and you hear screams coming from the other side of the street. As you look over you see two teenage girls kicking and hitting an older man. It is quite vicious and as the man falls to the ground the girls carry on kicking him. Other passers-by are not helping and are carrying on as if nothing is happening. You have no mobile phone with you to call the police.

   What do you do?

5. You're due to play in the county football cup final and you know you're not well. For the first time ever, a scout from a Premier League club is going to attend and talent spot. You have been looking forward to this match for months and so far have been the star player of the year.

   Do you play on and jeopardize your team's chances?

Citizenship through informed and responsible action   © Folens (copiable page)

Resource 1.9: Your own moral dilemma

Working in groups, write your own original moral dilemma.

The dilemma cannot relate to personal experiences of people in the class, so NO anecdotes about things that have really happened to someone in your group! Write a new dilemma, based on the discussions you have had. This should be a dilemma that you would find it difficult to solve and one which may divide your group about the ideal outcome.

_____

_____

_____

_____

_____

_____

_____

_____

_____

_____

_____

_____

_____

_____

_____

_____

_____

_____

_____

_____

Resource 1.10: Cheap clothes

You used to spend most of your pocket money buying new clothes and were really happy when a new bargain clothes shop opened in your town. It was great for you and your friends, because it meant you could now buy a new outfit regularly without having to worry too much about the price.

One day, you're out shopping when you're given a leaflet saying that the new shop treats its workers unfairly. You feel uncomfortable about this, so when the opportunity to do a group project on human rights comes up at school you decide it's a good chance to find out more.

You do some research and find many of the clothes sold in high-street shops are stitched in sweatshops in poorer countries. You read one story about a young woman called Saida who works in a sweatshop in Bangladesh for three pence an hour sewing clothes for the same chain as the new shop. When a big order has to be completed, Saida is forced to work many hours of overtime, often late into the night without any extra pay and with no breaks. She's even seen some of her workmates collapse with exhaustion at their sewing machines. Saida's story has a big effect on you – you are the same age, yet your lives are so different. You guiltily realize your love of cheap clothes is partly responsible for her position.

On completing your project, you make a resolution never to buy products in the shops that use sweatshop labour. This is harder than you imagined, as most of the high-street shops can't guarantee they don't use sweatshops. Even so, you're determined to stick to your beliefs even if the ethically-produced clothes are more expensive.

One Saturday, your friend Sarah asks you to go shopping with her to buy a new coat. You haven't seen Sarah for a while – you've been friends since you were very young but she's now at a different school. On the bus on the way to the shops she confides that some older girls at school have been making nasty remarks about what she wears and that's the reason she wants the new coat.

You're worried that your friend is being bullied, but she seems confident that a new coat is the answer. However, Sarah only has £15 to spend. She can't ask her mum for more money because she's recently lost her job and money's very tight at the moment. Sarah is happy that the new shop is now open, so she'll be able to get the coat she wants with her money. You know that this shop exploits workers in poorer countries and last week you were outside handing out leaflets about their poor treatment of workers.

You're sure that if your friend had done the project with you she'd feel the same way, but you're not sure if you can explain it to her without preaching. What's more, Sarah is convinced that a new coat is the answer to the bullying she's been getting at school, and you can't think of anywhere else she'll get one for £15.

What do you do?

Citizenship through informed and responsible action

Resource 1.11: Twins

You are the mother of twins, a girl and a boy. You waited several years for children with your husband and when you finally became pregnant, you were both overjoyed. You named your children Lewis and Hazel.

The twins are now 14 years old. As they grow up, you realize that there is a distinct difference in the way that your husband treats the children. To Lewis, he is warm, caring, loving and interested in every stage of his development. He spends a lot of time with your son and often takes him out for the day. He watches football with him every weekend, knows all of Lewis' friends by name and is very close to his son. Your daughter Hazel is much less interesting to him. He spends very little time with her and feels that raising her is her mother's job. Hazel is quieter than her brother, and you have noticed on many occasions that she tries to gain your husband's attention and seek his approval, but he seems unaware or disinterested. You have spoken to your husband on many occasions about his different treatment of the twins but he feels that it is a man's responsibility to raise his son. You cannot fault him as a husband or as a father to your son. Lewis adores him and he is generous and giving with his time and with his money.

You worry that Hazel is losing the little confidence she once had. She is angry and resentful about the different treatment they receive at home. She is starting to rebel in small ways and is growing apart from everyone else in the family. She is not close to Lewis and can be very rude and dismissive of him. She has also distanced herself from you and is no longer interested in the separate mother/daughter outings you organized to compensate for your husband's lack of attention.

Your husband has noticed Hazel's negative change in attitude, but blames you entirely for bad parenting and cannot see that he may be part of the problem. You love your husband very much and have no intention of leaving him, but it is breaking your heart to see the effect his indifference is having on your daughter.

What do you do?

Resource 1.12: Debating
controversial issues

You are going to take part in a debate on a controversial issue given to you by your teacher. Decide on a group leader and then spend five minutes preparing for 'battle'. You need to give a more convincing argument than the other team, and to prepare as many arguments as possible to support your case in order to win.

During the battle, each team takes it in turns to present an argument. Everyone should make one point and no one can speak more than twice.

This task is about teamwork! You will have to work together quickly to ensure every group member knows what to say and feels equipped with a pertinent point of view. Make sure all team members have a point written in the box below that they will feel comfortable making in the debate.

My argument

Theme two
Individuals and action

This theme starts to move the students from thinking just about their own identity to realizing that identity is linked to politics, power and sometimes abuse of power. One of the lessons requires a degree of enforced detachment from the class that some students and teachers may find difficult. However, in order for the best results to be achieved, it is important to try this different approach.

This theme also examines the contentious issue of stereotyping. This issue angers young people more than most and yet most students are guilty of practising it themselves, however unwittingly! The work on power and powerlessness uses the example of a young and struggling teacher. The work is designed to encourage the students to examine how the balance of power is structured in the classroom and how their own behaviour may sometimes affect teaching and learning.

Students are then introduced to different forms of action and asked which are most appropriate in different situations. The concept of consensus is introduced and young people are asked to examine 'social norms' in different time periods to establish the difference between 'social norms' and 'moral acceptability'. Through the lens of capital punishment, students consider consensus and whether or when this should be challenged.

Theme aims:

- To recognize that power relationships exist and can be abused.
- To understand how identity can be linked to power.
- To explore the dangers of stereotyping.
- To evaluate different forms of action.

Lesson One: Stereotypes

Learning objectives:

- To recognize the negative effects of stereotyping
- To understand that different 'social groups' exist, but that they overlap and are not definitive.

Resources: 2.1, 2.2, 2.3

Starter:
Divide students into four groups based on their birthdays as follows:

- January–March (winter)
- April–June (spring)
- July–September (summer)
- October–December (autumn)

Prepare four tables before the lesson, each with a sign naming the group ('Spring', 'Summer', 'Autumn' or 'Winter'). The division should feel as random and trivial as possible; this is just an arbitrary means of separating the class into unnatural groups.

As the class arrives, give each student a piece of card with the name of their birthday group on it and tell them to sit with others on the table that is labelled with their birthday season. You need to behave in a detached manner during this method of separation with no allowance for negotiation or humour. Students will question what is happening and try to resist separation that feels unnecessary or unnatural to them. Do not engage in justification; just point to where they are to sit. The key to this lesson is to remove the individual and interpersonal interactions that make lessons more interesting.

Throughout the lesson, whenever you refer to a student use the name from the table as a prefix and then the gender of the student as the suffix. For example:

Student: "Sir, please can I go to the toilet?"

Teacher: "**Spring Boy**, you may go at break."

You MUST avoid referring to students by their names at any point. There should be no acknowledgement of individuals' viewpoints or characteristics. You must be quite distant and authoritative in your manner. Think of the quizmaster in *University Challenge* or *The Weakest Link*! Do not respond personally or engage in chatting with your students. The idea is to challenge the usual group dynamics and to produce tension and resistance in your students.

On each table place the list of eight 'stereotypical' character traits for each group given on Resource 2.1. These are invented and intended to be as random and ridiculous as possible.

Main activity:
Each group must now produce a character that embodies all the traits of the group. The character must have a name, a back-story and a statement in her/his own words about her/his ambitions and expectations. Make sure each group has a box of art resources, some newspaper clippings, some fabrics, coloured paper, scissors, glue and so on. They also need a sheet of A2 paper. Ask each group to come to the front of the classroom to display their character and present their stereotypical creation.

When students have presented their characters, facilitate a discussion about why it might be harmful to imagine you know about someone because of their name, age, race or religion.

Using Resource 2.2 or other examples of your choice, ask students, still in their birthday groups, to think of five stereotypes for each social group. Then ask each group to read out their stereotypes and their exceptions, comparing them with the rest of the class.

Plenary:
Ask students how it felt to be segregated. Did you like it? Was it fair? How did it feel to be told at the start of the lesson what your traits were and how you would behave, based on something as arbitrary as your date of birth? Is this any sillier than thinking we know someone because of their gender, country of birth or their race or religion?

Extension activity:
Ask students to use Resource 2.3 to identify the different 'tribes' in their school, and the stereotypes associated with each of them.

Lesson Two: Power and the powerful

Learning objectives:
- To explore the definition of 'power' and our understandings of where power is located
- To recognize that individuals we think are powerful may themselves feel powerless
- To understand how individuals can act to change power structures.

Resources: 2.4, 2.5, 2.6, 2.7

Starter:
Ask students, in pairs, to draw a picture of a real person in the frame on Resource 2.4, listing five attributes that give that person power. They should spend five minutes on this before feeding back; create a list of all the power attributes on the board. If students need help to get them started, suggest Elizabeth II, Queen of England, who is powerful because she has money, status, servants, land and many supporters.

Facilitate a whole class discussion about where power comes from. Were there any attributes that came up more often than others? Does power always comes from the same source(s)?

Main activity:
Divide the class into two different groups. Give each group a different Rosie scenario from Resource 2.5. Each group must elect someone to read out the story of Rosie twice. Ideally the two groups should not be able to hear each other's versions of the same story. Each group should also elect a scribe to write down their agreed collective responses to each question on Resource 2.6. The groups are then given the alternative Rosie scenario.

You should facilitate a whole-class discussion around the questions, seeing if both groups agreed in their discussions about both sides of the argument.

Cut out the character cards from Resource 2.7 and assign each student a different character to inhabit. Place Rosie in the centre of the room and ask the other characters to stand as close, or as far away from her, as they think they are in helping her to 'gain power' and improve her classroom situation. Ask each character in the role play to explain what they think about Rosie and how they believe she could best help herself move out of her current situation.

Extension activity:
Ask students to write down five action points for Rosie to help her regain some power and respect from her students.

Lesson Three: Appropriate action

Learning objectives:

- To explore examples of different courses of action taken by individuals and groups to create change
- To recognize the different courses of action that can be taken to oppose or protest about an issue
- To identify key individuals with the ability to influence change in given situations
- To understand the consequences of different forms of action, considering how they influence individuals and the possible negative outcomes.

Resources: 2.8, 2.9, 2.10, 2.11, 2.12, 2.13

Starter:
Ask the class: 'Who creates change? The government or ordinary people?' Have a five-minute class discussion.

Main activity:
In pairs, ask students to read through the case studies about Gandhi and Che Guevara on Resource 2.8, then write their answers to the three questions.

In pairs, ask students to read through the case studies about the Iraq War protest and the G20 protests on Resource 2.9, then write their answers to the three questions.

Ask students to feed back their thoughts about each of the case studies and facilitate a class discussion using the following questions for inspiration:

- To create change you can try to influence the people who have authority. But is it equally important to influence those who don't have authority?
- Is it more important for many 'ordinary' people to support a cause, or a few people with 'authority'?

Divide students into groups of three or four. Cut out the scenario cards on Resource 2.10 and give one scenario to each group. Ask students to identify four key individuals who can influence change in their scenario and then complete the table on Resource 2.11.

Ask the groups to feed back to the class, describing their characters, the reasons they assigned the colours to each character, and how they would convince each of them to act.

Students must now devise a plan of appropriate action for each scenario based on the courses of action described in Resource 2.12 and write their answers in the table provided on Resource 2.13.

Plenary:
Ask the students to the debate the question: Is violent/destructive action ever justified?

Lesson Four: Challenging consensus

Learning objectives:

- To explore the arguments for and against capital punishment
- To recognize that different types of arguments will influence people with differing results
- To build a case based around an argument with which we may not agree.

Resource: 2.14

Starter:
Start the lesson by introducing the word 'galvanize', meaning to spur people into action. Explain that this lesson will be about how you motivate people and convince others that your argument, campaign or project is important enough for them to take action.

Main activity:
Use the following statements to lead an agree/disagree game:

1. The death penalty should be reintroduced in Britain.
2. Giving a murderer the death sentence will stop them doing it again, and deter others.
3. The death penalty goes against our most basic human right, the right to life.
4. If the wrong person is convicted an innocent person will be killed, and death cannot be reversed. In the USA, newly available DNA evidence has meant that some people who were executed were later found to be innocent.
5. No one has ever proven statistically that killing murderers stops other people committing similar crimes.
6. The punishment should fit the crime. If you have killed someone, you should be killed too.
7. Seventy-one countries retain and use the death penalty. The four countries with the largest populations (China, India, USA, Indonesia) apply the death penalty.
8. An eye for an eye makes the whole world blind.
9. The death penalty is cruel, inhuman and degrading.
10. The very small chance of executing the wrong person is balanced by the benefits to society of putting off other murderers.
11. If someone murders someone else, they have given up their human rights, including the right to stay alive themselves.
12. Support for the death penalty can be found in scriptures from different religions.
13. The death penalty is more expensive than life imprisonment.
14. The death penalty is often used disproportionately against the poor, minorities and members of racial, ethnic and religious communities.
15. In arguments about the death penalty, there are two lives to think about. Too much emphasis is placed on the rights of the convicted murderer, the one being executed, and the victim is forgotten.

This activity works best when there is plenty of space. This could be a good lesson to relocate to a drama space or to a school hall. Failing that, clear away all chairs and tables to enable the maximum amount of space for the activity.

Mark out a scale along one side of the room with 'AGREE' at one end and 'DISAGREE' at the other.

Introduce the topic to the class and then, as you read through each statement, ask students to position themselves on the scale to show how far they agree/disagree. So if they are completely unsure they stand in the middle, agree slightly and they move a few steps towards 'AGREE'. Students should move up and down the scale in response to each statement if it is powerful enough to make them change their view. They should not see the statements before they are read out, and should respond quickly and decisively to each.

After the game, ask the students which statements made most people move. Were there any types of statements that were more effective, such as those based on fact, emotion or the notion of human rights?

Working in groups of five, ask students to read through Brian's story on Resource 2.14. They then move on to the task, which is to write a speech to save Brian from the death sentence. The speech must be no more than three minutes long and the group must elect one person to deliver it to the class.

Plenary:
Instruct students to finish and practice their speeches in preparation for the next lesson.

Lesson Five: Challenging 'norms'

Learning objectives:

- To persuade others by delivering an argument in the form of a speech
- To recognize a 'norm' and to understand the factors that influence what we see as normal
- To understand that norms can change over time and to identify ways individuals and groups can influence change.

Resources: 2.15, 2.16 (CD-ROM only), 2.17, 2.18

Starter:
Groups deliver their speeches to save Brian from the death sentence. Elect three class members to act as the Supreme Court, which will make the final decision about which of the defence lawyers were successful in saving their client's life at the end of the session. The decision should be based only on the arguments they hear.

Main activity:
Ask the class to explain what we mean by a 'norm', using the notes below for guidance, and explain that this part of the lesson will be about challenging what we understand as normal in our everyday lives.

- A 'norm' or 'social norm' is a term used to describe the way a society or group of people is expected to behave.
- A norm guides which values, beliefs, behaviours or attitudes are appropriate; and also the way that people speak, dress and present themselves.
- Failure to stick to the norms can result in severe punishment, the worst being exclusion from the group.
- Norms vary between different age groups, social groups and cultures and evolve over time. They tell us what is considered 'normal' to a certain group of people at a certain time or in a certain place.

Ask students to work individually through the list on Resource 2.15 and decide how normal they think the action described in each statement is, marking their decision on the continuum.

Then ask them to feed back their decisions for each statement. You might want to draw a continuum on the board and ask class members to come up and mark on their answers. Facilitate a discussion on where each example might be considered normal/not normal, using the points below for guidance. Ask students what factors influenced their decisions about whether something was normal or not. Which factors – such as country, culture, context, age group, historical period and so on – would make them change the position on the continuum in each case?

1. Is it normal for people to live to at least 60?

Perhaps in the UK, where the average life expectancy is to live to your late 70s. But in other countries life expectancy is much lower. For example, in Angola it is 38.2.

2. Is it normal to eat three meals a day?

It might be normal for you, but in many countries the daily calorie intake is far lower than in the UK.

3. Is it normal to drink alcohol even if you are under-age?

Although it is illegal, many under-18s still drink alcohol in the UK and it is considered normal. In certain countries, such as Saudi Arabia, drinking alcohol is completely forbidden for people of all ages.

4. Is it normal to use a mobile phone?

In 2009, over 50 per cent of the world's population uses a mobile phone. By the end of 2008 there was an estimated 4.1 billion mobile subscriptions.

5. Is it normal for adults to listen to young people's views?

Today we hope adults listen to young people and care what they think! However, in the past children were encouraged to be 'seen and not heard'.

6. Is it normal to have access to free health care?

In the UK everyone is entitled to free health care through the National Health Service (NHS). In the USA and many other countries around the world, this is not the case.

7. Is it normal to be free to criticize the government?

In the UK today, journalists are free to criticize the government if they choose to. In Eritrea, for example, independent and private journalism is prohibited and you can be put in prison for writing against the government.

8. Is it normal to forbid parents to have more than one child?

In the UK, parents can have as many children as they want. Some countries have rules for how many children a couple can have. In China, the 'one-child policy' was introduced in 1979. It means that married couples can only have one child, to limit population growth.

Draw a timeline stretching from 1800 to the present on the board or project Resource 2.16. Each student needs to be handed one of the cards from Resource 2.17 and a piece of Blu-Tack®. They must then come up to the board and place the card at the point they think it should go – the most recent point this action was considered normal. When all the cards have been placed, show the class the correct timeline on Resource 2.18.

Plenary:
Ask students: What surprised you? Just because we see something as normal, does it mean it can't be changed?

Extension activity:
Ask students to carry out research and complete the empty 'Explanation' boxes on Resource 2.18, to explain why the norms highlighted changed.

Resource 2.1: Stereotypical character traits

Winter	Spring
Selfish	Bad at spelling
Good business sense	Generous
Well-organized	No fashion sense
No sense of humour	Easily influenced by others
Loves animals	Loves a good laugh
Can be vain	Always singing
Self-reliant	Rarely on time
Cautious	Curly hair
Summer	**Autumn**
Not to be trusted	Good at map reading
Popular	Softly spoken
Carefree	Can be moody
Low academic ability	Likes wearing hats
No books in their home	Perfectionist
Good at physical activities	Snobbish
Strong sense of fashion	Only child
Wide feet	Strong academic ability

Resource 2.2: Stereotypes

Write down five stereotypes for each group below. When you have finished, have some fun in sharing and comparing the stereotypes.

Then, see if you can think of an individual that would be an exception to the stereotypical list, such as a highly-educated and articulate footballer or an honest and likeable politician?

Footballers	**The Royal family**
1. _____	1. _____
2. _____	2. _____
3. _____	3. _____
4. _____	4. _____
5. _____	5. _____
Any exceptions?	Any exceptions?
_____	_____
_____	_____
Actors	**Politicians**
1. _____	1. _____
2. _____	2. _____
3. _____	3. _____
4. _____	4. _____
5. _____	5. _____
Any exceptions?	Any exceptions?
_____	_____
_____	_____

Resource 2.3: Tribes

Think of three different 'tribes' that exist in your school. These should be groups that are seen as sharing certain values, attributes or interests, that may be labelled by themselves or others.

List five stereotypes that exist about each group.

Tribe 1:	Stereotypes: • _____ • _____ • _____ • _____ • _____
Tribe 2:	Stereotypes: • _____ • _____ • _____ • _____ • _____
Tribe 3:	Stereotypes: • _____ • _____ • _____ • _____ • _____

Resource 2.4: Power attributes

Draw a picture of a real person you think is powerful in the space provided. Write your chosen person's name and a brief explanation of who they are. Then, list five attributes that give this person power.

Name: _____

Who am I? _____

Power attributes:

1. _____
_____
_____
_____

2. _____
_____
_____
_____

3. _____
_____
_____
_____

4. _____
_____
_____
_____

5. _____
_____
_____
_____

Resource 2.5: Power vs. powerless

Rosie 1

Rosie is a 27-year-old English teacher. She has been in her current job for two years and is achieving high grades with her GCSE classes. She is very strict with her students and shouts at them a lot if they misbehave. The students in her classes are not fond of her at all, but they know that she will ensure they achieve good grades in their GCSE exams.

Rosie is obsessed with her classes being still and quiet at all times and prevents her students getting involved in drama or role plays or many of the activities that would make her lessons more fun.

Rosie doesn't deal well with comments from the students and becomes angry when they ask her personal questions about her home life, such as whether she has children or whether she enjoyed school herself. Her students are trying to get to know her a little better and they feel that she can be cold and sharp with them. It is obvious she really doesn't like children.

Rosie is impatient and makes the class leave her classroom within two minutes of the bell ringing. She won't allow computers in her classroom like the other English teachers do and she always chooses the English texts that other teachers avoid because they are harder or take longer to read.

Rosie tends to go very red in the face when she is angry and this can lead to some of the students drawing caricatures of her or impersonating her behind her back. She does not command the respect of the class and is therefore not a good teacher.

Rosie 2

Rosie is a 27-year-old English teacher. She has been in her current job for two years and is desperate to hold onto it as she knows that the Head teacher's daughter has recently qualified as an English teacher and the Head would like to bring her to his school to work. She spends most evenings working until 11pm, marking books, preparing lessons and ensuring that the Head teacher cannot fault any of her lessons if he were to walk into her classroom. Which he does, frequently.

Rosie is aware that the students in her class don't like her. She has always had a huge problem with confidence and she masks this by pretending to be assertive and shouting, rather than letting people see her fear. Rosie came from a difficult background: she is one of seven children and she was the only one to go to university. She is now financially responsible for looking after her mother and three of her younger sisters, all of whom live in her house and do not work.

Rosie is intimidated by the confidence shown by some of the students she teaches. She is worried about allowing them to take part in drama or role plays, as this would mean she would not be in control of the class. She avoids using computers in her classroom as she is embarrassed to admit that she has no idea how to use one and has never had one in her home.

Rosie knows students draw caricatures of her. She found one and kept it to remind herself that she has a long way to go as a teacher. She makes the class leave on the bell, as she finds teaching really stressful and is often close to tears at the end of the lesson.

Resource 2.8: Revolutionaries

A revolutionary is someone who supports abrupt, rapid, and drastic change. Here are the stories of two revolutionaries with very different approaches. Read the stories and answer the questions below.

Gandhi

Mohandas Karamchand Gandhi (2 October 1869–30 January 1948) was a political and spiritual leader. He led India to independence from the British Empire by a process of non-violent civil disobedience. He is commonly known around the world as Mahatma Gandhi and is officially honoured in India as the 'Father of the Nation'. 'Mahatma' means 'Great Soul' in Sanskrit.

Gandhi led nationwide campaigns for combatting poverty, expanding women's rights, building religious and ethnic harmony, and above all independence for India from foreign control. Gandhi employed non-violent non-cooperation and peaceful resistance as his 'weapons' in the struggle against the British. In addition to boycotting British products, Gandhi urged the Indian people to boycott British educational institutions and law courts, to reject British titles and honours, and to resign from jobs in the government.

Gandhi was shot and killed on 30 January 1948, by a young Hindu fanatic.

Gandhi is celebrated worldwide as an example of what you can achieve without resorting to violence.

Che Guevara

Ernesto 'Che' Guevara (14 June 1928–9 October 1967) was an Argentine revolutionary, politician and guerrilla leader. After his death, his image became a worldwide icon for revolution – you've probably seen his face on a T-shirt!

He played a pivotal role in the Cuban revolution, overthrowing the dictator Fulgencio Batista through a successful two-year guerrilla campaign. His commanding officer, Fidel Castro, described Guevara as intelligent, daring and an exemplary leader who 'had great moral authority over his troops'.

Guevara thought that the only answer to poverty was world revolution. He was both dedicated and ruthless in this quest, using violent means where he saw fit, shooting those he considered traitors or war criminals.

1. Is Che Guevara more famous for his looks or his actions?
2. Do either of these figures have 'moral superiority'?
3. Do their actions hold any relevance for us today?

Protest against the Iraq War

The 15 February 2003 anti-war protest was a day of protests across the world against the invasion of Iraq. Protests happened in around 800 cities around the world with an estimated 6 million–30 million people protesting.

Some of the largest protests took place in Europe. The protest in Rome involved around three million people and is listed in the 2004 *Guinness Book of World Records* as the largest anti-war rally in history.

Despite these protests, the war went ahead. However, the fact that a huge number of people demonstrated publicly they did not approve of the war showed governments around the world that the war was not backed by everyone.

The G20 protests

The G20 Leaders' Summit was a meeting of world leaders to discuss the global economy. It was held in London, on 2 April 2009.

Demonstrations happened across London before the summit was held, the main protests taking place on 1 April 2009. People wanted to protest about a range of issues, calling for an end to poverty, action on climate change, nuclear disarmament, and to express their dissatisfaction with the handling of the economy.

The 1 April 2009 protests were for the most part peaceful with some outbreaks of disorder. Climate change activists pitched

tents in the street, while anti-war campaigners held a rally. Some demonstrators launched missiles and forced their way into the Royal Bank of Scotland after clashes with police. A branch of HSBC also had its windows smashed. Police cordoned off large numbers of the protesters outside the Bank of England, and held them there for up to seven hours. There were 63 arrests on the day. Some police and protesters were injured, and one man died after collapsing within a police cordon set up to contain the crowds who had assembled to protest.

1. At what point does legal protest become civil disobedience?
2. Considering the Iraq War went ahead, despite the millions of people who marched against it, was there any point in protesting?
3. Do governments or political parties pay any attention to mass protest?

Homophobic chanting at a local football match.	A supermarket uses sweatshop labour in a developing country to produce its clothes.
An animal testing centre is due to be built next to your school. The centre will test cosmetic products only.	Too many people drive to work in a small town instead of using public transport or car sharing.
A school nurse is sacked after a local newspaper reported she gave condoms to students over the age of consent in a Catholic school.	A local specialist school for children with disabilities is due to be closed down.

Resource 2.11: Individuals and power

1. In your group, decide on four key individuals that have the power to change the situation in your scenario.
2. When you have your four characters, give each a colour rating:

   - red = lots of power
   - yellow = some power
   - blue = not very powerful

3. Look at each character and decide what would be the best way to convince them to use their power to change the situation.

Scenario:

Key individual	Power rating (red/yellow/blue)	How could you convince them to change the situation?

Which of the following forms of protest would be suitable for your scenario?

Sit-in People occupy an area and remain seated until they are evicted, usually by force, or until their requests have been met.	**Soapbox** A raised platform which is stood on to make a public speech.
Raasta roko People block traffic with their bodies.	**Graffiti** Images or lettering painted or scratched into property to communicate a message.
Peace camp A campsite set up outside a military base to oppose war.	**Letter writing** Writing letters to register a protest.
Riot A sudden demonstration of violence involving vandalism and the destruction of private and public property.	**Consumer boycott** People stop using, or buying from a particular shop or company.
Public nudity Sometimes used to attract more attention to a public protest.	**Facebook campaign** Using the social networking site to gather supporters.
'Die-in' Protesters lie down on the ground and pretend to be dead, sometimes covering themselves with signs or banners.	**Picket** People congregate outside a place of work or location where an event is taking place, often with large placards or signs. This might be to stop others from going in or to draw public attention to a cause.
Walkout Students or workers all leave their place of work or school at the same time.	**Protest march** A demonstration where a group of people walk in a large group, often holding placards.
Hunger strike People fast or go without food, to shame or embarrass others into action.	**Petition** A collection of signatures delivered to an official person, such as the local MP.

Resource 2.13: Pros and cons

Choose three forms of protest from Resource 2.12 that would be suitable for your scenario. Then list the pros and cons for each form of protest.

Scenario:		
Form of protest:	**Pros:**	**Cons:**
1.		
2.		
3.		

For example:

Scenario: *Homophobic chanting at a local football match*		
Form of protest:	**Pros:**	**Cons:**
1. *Graffiti anti–homophobia message around football ground.*	*Many people may see the message.*	*Involves vandalizing property, which is illegal so could get you arrested and alienate your intended audience.*

Resource 2.14: Death penalty defence

Read Brian's story and then complete the task below.

Brian's story

Brian was born into a poor family in Texas, USA. He never knew his father. His stepdad was violent towards him constantly and his mother felt powerless to stop the beating as she was often attacked by her husband herself. Brian excelled at American football at school but failed in most other subjects. Brian dropped out of school after a fight in which he broke the teeth of another boy who had called him a 'hillbilly tramp'.

Brian's mother died aged 38 and his stepdad inherited the house and immediately kicked Brian and his brother out. Brian worked in lots of low-paid jobs, but he usually ended up getting fired through lateness or his temper.

Brian, now aged 19, was sleeping rough and using a lot of drugs. He did not look after himself and he became known to the police because of his violent behaviour and his short temper. He was arrested on several occasions and was usually drunk and disorderly. His old friends no longer wished to associate with him as he was constantly in trouble and his personal hygiene was now so poor that he smelt bad.

His old football coach, Sam Metcalfe, saw him on the street and offered him a place in his house to 'shape up and sort out his life'. Brian stayed in the house for three months, attended rehab classes and came off the drugs. He worked around the house and looked after the garden as he had no money for rent. It was the happiest period of his life. Then Sam had a huge stroke and was hospitalized. His wife had never felt particularly comfortable with Brian in the house and used this opportunity to tell him to leave. Brian begged and pleaded with her but she made him pack his bag and leave.

Brian packed his bag. He then walked downstairs and strangled Mrs Metcalfe in her kitchen. He left a note for Sam on the table saying that he was sorry and then went down to the river and threw himself off a bridge. A passer-by pulled him from the river and the police arrested him shortly afterwards. Sam Metcalfe died in hospital, shortly after hearing about his wife's murder. After a long trial, Brian was given the death penalty for the murder of Mrs Metcalfe, which he admitted. Brian claims it was just the final straw and that he committed the crime out of desperation and frustration. Brian is scheduled to die in the electric chair next Wednesday, after spending two years on death row. He has received no visitors in this time. He is now aged 22.

You are Brian's defence lawyers and you have to make the speech of your life to defend Brian in front of a judge and jury to try and save his life. You have to convince the jury that the death penalty is not the correct punishment for Brian. You can use any of the information from his story above to strengthen your case.

You should work in groups and nominate one person to deliver the speech to the rest of the class. The speech must be written up by your group and handed in to your teacher as evidence. The speech must be less than three minutes long.

Citizenship through informed and responsible action © Folens (copiable page)

Resource 2.15: What is normal?

Read through the questions below and consider how normal the action is. Mark your decision in the appropriate place on the scale.

1. Is it normal for people to live to at least 60?

NORMAL ◄――――――――――――――――――――――――――――――► **ABNORMAL**

2. Is it normal to eat three meals a day?

NORMAL ◄――――――――――――――――――――――――――――――► **ABNORMAL**

3. Is it normal to drink alcohol even if you are under-age?

NORMAL ◄――――――――――――――――――――――――――――――► **ABNORMAL**

4. Is it normal to use a mobile phone?

NORMAL ◄――――――――――――――――――――――――――――――► **ABNORMAL**

5. Is it normal for adults to listen to young people's views?

NORMAL ◄――――――――――――――――――――――――――――――► **ABNORMAL**

6. Is it normal to have access to free health care?

NORMAL ◄――――――――――――――――――――――――――――――► **ABNORMAL**

7. Is it normal to be free to criticize the government?

NORMAL ◄――――――――――――――――――――――――――――――► **ABNORMAL**

8. Is it normal to forbid parents to have more than one child?

NORMAL ◄――――――――――――――――――――――――――――――► **ABNORMAL**

Women have equal voting rights with men.

Shops can't open on a Sunday.

Children under the age of 12 work as chimney sweeps.

Opium is used as a medicine by most families during the nineteenth century.

Homosexuality is illegal.

Women are allowed in the army.

Women prisoners are handcuffed during childbirth.

Most household waste is recycled.

Resource 2.18: Timeline

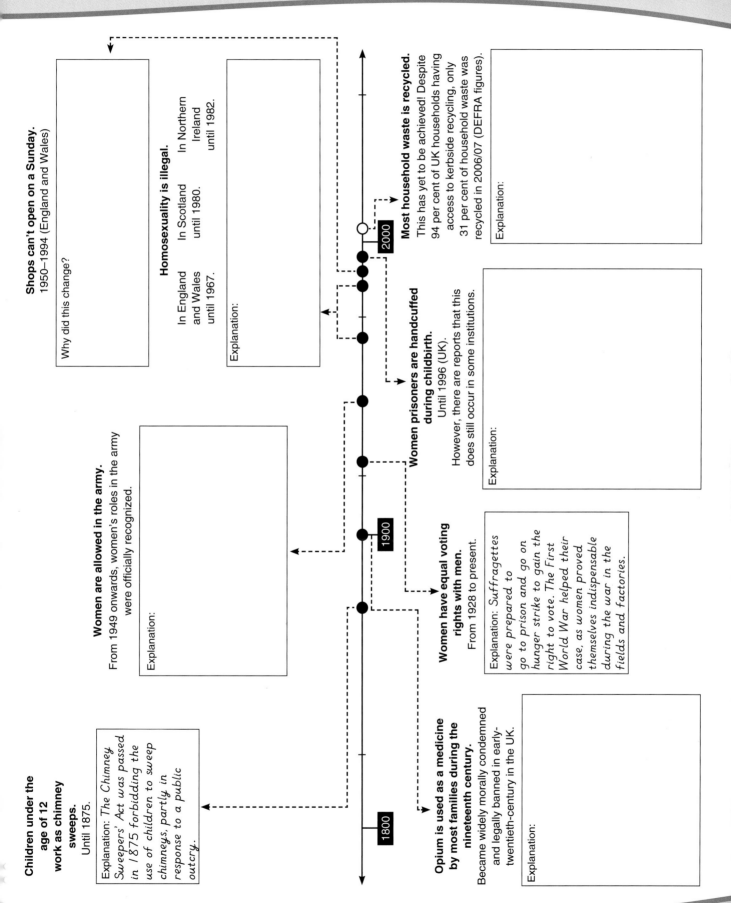

Shops can't open on a Sunday.
1950–1994 (England and Wales)

Why did this change?

Homosexuality is illegal.

In England and Wales until 1967.

In Scotland until 1980.

In Northern Ireland until 1982.

Explanation:

Most household waste is recycled.
This has yet to be achieved! Despite 94 per cent of UK households having access to kerbside recycling, only 31 per cent of household waste was recycled in 2006/07 (DEFRA figures).

Explanation:

2000

Women prisoners are handcuffed during childbirth.
Until 1996 (UK).
However, there are reports that this does still occur in some institutions.

Explanation:

Women are allowed in the army.
From 1949 onwards, women's roles in the army were officially recognized.

Explanation:

1900

Women have equal voting rights with men.
From 1928 to present.

Explanation: *Suffragettes were prepared to go to prison and go on hunger strike to gain the right to vote. The First World War helped their case, as women proved themselves indispensable during the war in the fields and factories.*

Children under the age of 12 work as chimney sweeps.
Until 1875.

Explanation: *The Chimney Sweepers' Act was passed in 1875 forbidding the use of children to sweep chimneys, partly in response to a public outcry.*

Opium is used as a medicine by most families during the nineteenth century.
Became widely morally condemned and legally banned in early-twentieth-century in the UK.

Explanation:

1800

Theme three
Persuasion and influence

The main focus of this theme is the way in which words can be used to persuade others and influence situations to bring about change or oppose a situation. The theme looks at the spoken word, considering how young people and adults communicate and how the words we choose, and the way we deliver them, can lead to misunderstanding.

There are exercises provided to encourage young people to think about how they need to 'refine' their voice so that it is more effective in achieving their aims, especially when aiming to influence adults.

The students have an opportunity to analyse a famous modern speech and understand what makes the speech effective and to identify the intended outcomes for the speaker. By this point, the young people should be confident in speaking out in classroom situations, debating with their peers and challenging lazy assumptions. The interaction between young people and the rest of British society is a pertinent issue and one that provokes strong debate among students. This is an ideal opportunity to discuss notions of British citizenship and how it applies specifically to young people. Does society allow enough opportunities for active and sustained Citizenship?

At a time when the digital age is having an influence over levels of literacy, the final task is for students to master the written word and to write a letter of influence, to an appropriate individual or organization, about an issue that concerns them.

Theme aims:

- To examine the role of language in persuading and influencing others.
- To introduce students to a range of communication tools.
- To provide opportunities for students to use their voice appropriately.

Lesson One: Speaking to adults

Learning objectives:

- To identify the differences in the ways young people and adults communicate, recognizing areas that might lead to misunderstanding
- To gain the skills needed to communicate with adults about sensitive issues, in order to obtain a positive outcome.

Resources: 3.1, 3.2, 3.3

Starter:
Write the two following questions on the board for discussion:

- Is text speak killing young people's ability to communicate effectively?
- Is text speak a young person's way of keeping adults out of their conversations?

Have a ten-minute whole-class discussion around these two questions, encouraging as many students as possible to get involved.

Main activity:

Ask students, in pairs, to read through the scenario on Resource 3.1 about an adult being dismissive towards a young person who needs their help, one playing Toni and one playing the receptionist. They must then rewrite the scenario so the characters communicate differently to come to a more positive conclusion.

In pairs, ask students to read through one of the scenarios on Resource 3.2 or 3.3 where a young person needs to speak to an adult about a sensitive issue. They need to look at the four different ways the young person approaches the issue and answer the three questions.

You could then ask students to role play each of these scenarios. They should change the dilemma's wording/ setting/characters if necessary, but ensure they work out what would be the best way of approaching each issue in order to get the best outcome.

Plenary:

Facilitate a class discussion, asking students if they have ever felt unwelcome in an adult environment or have struggled to be taken seriously by adults.

Lesson Two: The power of the word

Learning objectives:

- To gain the skills to use the written word in order to persuade others to take a certain course of action
- To analyse a text to understand how spoken words can be used with impact
- To understand the elements necessary to write a powerful speech.

Resources: 3.4, 3.5 (CD-ROM only), 3.6

Starter:

Ask students to spend five minutes writing a paragraph persuading you not to give them homework. If they are successful and their paragraphs are persuasive enough – no homework!

Main activity:

Give each student a copy of the eulogy given by Earl Spencer at the funeral of Diana, Princess of Wales (Resource 3.4). The full transcript of the speech is provided on Resource 3.5 (CD-ROM), which you may want to give to higher-attaining students. You may also want to show footage of the speech. Before asking students to read the speech, explain some of the background to it:

Diana, Princess of Wales, was the first wife of Prince Charles. Their sons, Prince William and Prince Harry, are second and third in line to the throne of the United Kingdom. Diana was a high-profile public figure from the announcement of her engagement to Prince Charles. She was constantly scrutinized by the media in the United Kingdom and around the world up to and during her marriage, and after her subsequent divorce.

She died suddenly in a car crash in Paris in 1997, aged 36. Her death was followed by a spontaneous and prolonged show of public mourning. Her funeral saw a widespread outpouring of public grief. It was attended by members of the Royal family and was broadcast and watched by an estimated 2.5 billion people worldwide. During the service, Elton John sang a new version of *Candle In The Wind*, his hit song initially dedicated to Marilyn Monroe.

Students must then work through the textual analysis questions, individually writing the answers in their books.

Ask students to fill a page with words they think the British public uses to describe its young people. You could provide them with a large piece of paper or use the board and ask students to fill the space.

Provide students with Resource 3.6, which describes the 'Mosquito' device. They should read through it individually. They then need to read the speech prepared by a teenage boy about the device, and re-write the speech so that it will have more effect, using the pointers provided.

Plenary:
Facilitate a class discussion about how students feel Britain treats its young people.

Extension activity:
Encourage students to practise the new speech written in response to Resource 3.6 and select three volunteers to deliver their speeches to the class in the next lesson.

Lesson Three: Making a difference – what can you do?

Learning objectives:

- To understand the elements necessary to deliver a powerful speech
- To utilize and analyse a variety of sources to research an issue, and to use this research to inform arguments
- To gain the skills to write a persuasive letter.

Resources: 3.7, 3.8

Starter:
Students are to deliver their speech written in the previous lesson. Ask the class to identify which speeches were particularly successful, and highlight the elements in those that made them more effective.

Main activity:
In this lesson, students will choose a controversial issue (the last two are best aimed at KS4) from Resource 3.7 and, using the guidelines in Resource 3.8 write a persuasive letter on their chosen subject. Ideally, this lesson needs to be taught in a room with at least five computers available for student research. Tell the class they will now need to write a letter that persuades another person of their point of view. The aim of this task is to persuade someone who has influence to change the situation.

You may want to suggest appropriate individuals that students can contact for each issue, bearing in mind which contacts are more likely to write a response.

Extension activity:
Ask students to complete their letters and return them next lesson. Check letters before sending them, ensuring a return address has been included.

Resource 3.1: Getting what you want

Read through the following script.

A teenager called Toni walks into a social services office. She is extremely worried that her younger cousin is being abused by her new stepfather. She does not have strong family relationships in order to discuss this at home and wants to alert social services to the abuse.

She is a little intimidated by the adult environment, but goes to the front desk and asks for assistance.

Toni:	I need to talk to someone about my cousin.
Receptionist:	Have you booked an appointment? Can I take your name?
Toni:	(defensively) I don't want to give my name. I just came in because I was in town today, I didn't know you had to make appointments.
Receptionist:	Right, well the first thing you need to do is to ring and book an appointment with the relevant department.
Toni:	I don't know what department it is.
Receptionist:	Look on our social services website, that has everything outlined.
Toni:	I haven't got a computer; I don't have time to do that anyway, I just need to talk to someone here. (raising her voice) It's important.
Receptionist:	Maybe if you could come back another time when you know what you want and with an adult.
Toni:	I don't want to bring an adult, I can do it myself, I just don't know what to do. (becoming stressed and emotional) Why are you being like this?
Receptionist:	(impatient) I've given you all the help I can give you. There's a queue building up behind you. Please can you go home and find the details you need and then we can try this again another day. You need to understand the organization in order for us to progress your needs.
Toni:	Why are you being such a cow? I just need to talk to someone.
Receptionist:	I won't tolerate being abused by members of the public. I'm going to have to ask you to leave.
Toni:	Sorry but you weren't ...
Receptionist:	(calls) Security!

Now, on the back of this sheet, re-write this scene using the same characters in the same situation but allowing Toni to make her point in a manner that the receptionist finds acceptable and therefore leads to a more positive outcome.

Resource 3.2: Speaking to adults 1

Hannah's mum goes out socializing all the time with her friends. She is rarely around in the evenings to spend time with Hannah and her younger sister and she never has time to help Hannah with her homework. She often stays out late, leaving Hannah to look after her sister, and she is usually too tired in the morning to see them before school. Hannah wishes her mum would spend more time at home.

There are four ways that Hannah could tackle her mum about the situation:

a. 'You're never here! You're a bad parent and I hate it!'
b. 'You're neglecting your responsibilities as a parent.'
c. 'You're too old to be going out all the time, you and your stupid friends. It's embarrassing.'
d. 'We know seeing your friends is important to you, but we'd appreciate it if you were at home more. We miss you.'

1. How do you think Hannah's mum will respond to each of these statements?

2. Explain why each statement would or wouldn't work.

3. Which statement would produce the most positive response from Hannah's mum? How would Hannah's mum respond to it?

Citizenship through informed and responsible action

Resource 3.3: Speaking to adults 2

Callum is on his way to his final interview to join the Royal Air Force (RAF). There is only one bus an hour, and he's already late so he knows he has to run if he's going to make it on time. Just as he gets to the corner of the main road, Callum is stopped by a Police Community Support Officer. The officer asks him why he's in such a hurry and then begins to ask him a series of questions. Callum knows he'll miss the bus if he loses any more time and that the RAF won't accept lateness for any reason. What should he say?

There are four ways that Callum could respond:

a. (Interrupting) 'I ain't done nothing! What you hassling me for?'
b. 'Sorry, I'm just in a hurry because I need to get the bus. I've got an interview for the RAF. It's the 197 bus and it only runs once an hour.'
c. 'I didn't realize it was a crime to run. Shouldn't you be looking for actual criminals instead of wasting my time?'
d. 'I can't stop, I'm late. I haven't got time for this, can you just let me go?'

1. How do you think the PCSO will respond to each of these statements?

2. Explain why each statement would or wouldn't work.

3. Which statement would produce the most positive response from the PCSO? How would the PCSO respond to it?

Resource 3.4: Eulogy to Diana, Princess of Wales by the Earl Spencer (abridged)

Read through the following speech, made by Earl Spencer, Princess Diana's brother, at her funeral. Once you have read the speech, answer the questions below.

I stand before you today, the representative of a family in grief, in a country in mourning, before a world in shock. We are all united, not only in our desire to pay our respects to Diana, but rather in our need to do so. For such was her extraordinary appeal that the tens of millions of people taking part in this service all over the world via television and radio who never actually met her, feel that they too lost someone close to them in the early hours of Sunday morning. It is a more remarkable tribute to Diana than I can ever hope to offer her today.

Diana was the very essence of compassion, of duty, of style, of beauty.

…

And here we come to another truth about her. For all the status, the glamour, the applause, Diana remained throughout a very insecure person at heart, almost childlike in her desire to do good for others so she could release herself from deep feelings of unworthiness of which her eating disorders were merely a symptom.

The world sensed this part of her character and cherished her for her vulnerability whilst admiring her for her honesty.

…

These were days I will always treasure. It was as if had been transported back to our childhood when we spent such an enormous amount of time together – the two youngest in the family.

Fundamentally she had not changed at all from the big sister who mothered me as a baby, fought with me at school and endured those long train journeys between our parents' homes with me at weekends.

…

She talked endlessly of getting away from England, mainly because of the treatment that she received at the hands of the newspapers. I don't think she ever understood why her genuinely good intentions were sneered at by the media, why there appeared to be a permanent quest on their behalf to bring her down. It is baffling.

…

It is a point to remember that of all the ironies about Diana, perhaps the greatest was this: a girl given the name of the ancient goddess of hunting was, in the end, the most hunted person of the modern age.

She would want us today to pledge ourselves to protecting her beloved boys, William and Harry, from a similar fate, and I do this here, Diana, on your behalf.

We will not allow them to suffer the anguish that used regularly to drive you to tearful despair. And beyond that, on behalf of your mother and sisters, I pledge that we, your blood family, will do all we can to continue the imaginative way in which you were steering these two exceptional young men so that their souls are not simply immersed by duty and tradition but can sing openly as you planned.

…

William and Harry, we all care desperately for you today. We are all chewed up with sadness at the loss of a woman who was not even our mother. How great your suffering is we cannot even imagine.

…

Above all, we give thanks for the life of a woman I'm so proud to be able to call my sister, the unique, the complex, the extraordinary and irreplaceable Diana whose beauty, both internal and external, will never be extinguished from our minds.

Reproduced by the kind permission of the Earl Spencer

1. Who was the speech aimed at?
2. Which three sentences do you think are the most powerful and why?
3. What was Earl Spencer trying to achieve?
4. Where does he use emotion?
5. Where does he use anger?
6. Where does he use fact?
7. What impact do you think the speech had on the millions of members of the public who were listening across the UK and around the world?
8. What impression of Diana do you gain from this speech?
9. Is it a 'brave' speech? Why? Why not?
10. Why do you think this is ranked as one of the greatest speeches of modern times?

Citizenship through informed and responsible action   © Folens (copiable page)

Resource 3.6: The Mosquito

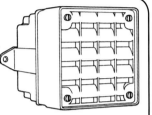

"Extensive research and development has produced the Mosquito device that uses complex high-frequency sound to chase away those annoying teenagers!"

A machine that emits an annoying sound that only youths can hear is being tested as a way to break up groups of loitering teens. Dubbed 'The Mosquito' by inventor Howard Stapleton, the machine looks like a box with a small loudspeaker attached. It can be mounted over the entrance to a store. A teenage boy described it as resembling "a violin string (being rubbed), but really, really, really high pitched." The sound is supposed to work as a repellent for the simple reason that most people over 30 can't hear it and most people under 20 can, and hate it.

A London teenager speaks in response to the story on their local news bulletin:

"I want to talk about an important issue. The Mosquito is used in some parts of Northern England in shops to deter young people from congregating in areas. This is blatantly unfair! Why should young people have to have their hearing affected in this way? There are teenagers who get headaches from these machines and that is surely not right, because the Mosquito machine is against their human rights. They should be removed from every shop NOW! It may not affect me and it may not affect you but we still need to stand strong and campaign against them because it is immoral that they should even exist."

The teenager's speech has a lot of passion, but the young person fails in many ways. How could you re-write the speech and make it far more likely to persuade people to stop using the Mosquito? What would you change and why?

Pointers:

- Make sure the argument is clear. What do you want the speech to achieve?
- Think about the audience: Who are you trying to persuade?
- Short sentences have more impact.
- Repetition can be effective. For example, Barack Obama's 'Yes We Can' (2008) and Tony Blair's 'Education, Education, Education' (1997)
- Start and finish on a strong point.

_____

_____

_____

_____

_____

_____

_____

_____

Resource 3.7: Controversial issues

Cheap clothing

What are the consequences of our high streets providing clothing at 'throwaway' prices on a local and global scale?

Smoking

Should people be given the free choice to smoke when all the evidence points to the fact that it leads to serious illness and early death?

Wealth and inequality

Is it right that, in British society, wealth enables you to purchase the best in public services, such as health care, legal representation and education?

Youth representation

Are young people unfairly represented in the media as only either the victims or perpetrators of crime?

Iraq War

What are the dangers in a government embarking on an unpopular war without the majority backing of the population?

Men's magazines

Should society make adult men's magazines so easily available when they contain images that many see as disrespectful/degrading to women?

Resource 3.8: Composing a persuasive letter

When writing a persuasive letter to a person of influence about a difficult subject, it is important to follow some key steps to ensure that your voice is heard:

Step five: Write your persuasive letter. Make sure this letter isn't just a rant and examines BOTH sides of the argument. State why you have written this letter and what your personal interest is in the issue. Keep the letter a reasonable length (no more than one page of A4) and ask for a response at the end. Show it to your teacher when you have finished it, prior to sending it off, for any feedback. Type it up and keep a copy for yourself so that you can re-send it to someone else if there is no response within four weeks.

Step four: Test out your argument on a tough audience. There is no point in just checking with a friend who shares your outlook. Push yourself and test your argument against someone who is likely to give you the reasons why your argument is wrong. Don't argue the importance of a smoke-free Britain with a non-smoker; argue the point with someone who may be elderly and has smoked all their life and can see nothing wrong in what they do. They will challenge you far more and therefore improve your letter.

Step three: Decide *who* your audience is. You want your letter to have an impact, so you need to ensure you send it to someone influential who can listen and then possibly make changes. It is no good just writing to someone involved in the issue, such as the manager of a high-street store, because they have less ability to challenge the use of sweatshops and child labour in India than the chief executive of the company. Think carefully and research who could support your cause or who could make a change. Perhaps this is a government minister or a charity connected with your chosen subject.

Step two: Research and support your thinking with FACTS to back up and strengthen your argument. It is not enough to just say that 'war is wrong'. Find backing from statistics that could justify your point about the cost in money and human misery. The inclusion of quotations from influential people, such as political leaders, heads of charities and those affected negatively by the issue, can also help your argument.

Step one: First, be sure of your own viewpoint! You cannot convince others if you are unsure yourself.

Theme four
The role of the media

If a campaign is to achieve some kind of change, the media needs to be engaged effectively to transmit the message. This theme asks students to evaluate exactly what role the media can play in achieving their aims and maximizing the audiences reached. Students are encouraged to understand the benefits of the media, but also to understand that the media has its own agenda and that this can be both unhelpful and unhealthy.

Students also examine how the media construct a story, which in turn determines which individuals or news stories receive the greatest amount of coverage. They are encouraged to look beyond headlines or the amount of space accorded a news story, to decide for themselves its true relevance or level of importance.

This theme also examines the local and international media and considers issues of political corruption. Students are encouraged to make a series of democratic decisions and consider the role of morality in the modern media.

Theme aims:

- To recognize the power of the media and how they influence people's opinions.
- To investigate the role the media can play in galvanizing a successful campaign.
- To debate the role of morality in the modern media.

Lesson One: Making headlines

Learning objectives:

- To understand that media coverage can be biased
- To recognize that the media can influence which issues the public sees as important
- To explore the ways the media can influence our perception of public figures.

Resources: 4.1, 4.2

Starter:
Ask students to write a list of the types of stories most often reported in the popular tabloid newspapers. Examples of popular stories might include: anything to do with celebrities, those who wish to attack Britain/British values, violent crime, immigration.

When students have written their own answers, facilitate a class discussion around the question: Do we decide what is important enough to make the headlines, or do the media decide what is important in society for us?

Main activity:
Students should read through the two examples of stories widely reported on by the media on Resource 4.1 and identify the 'ingredients' in each case that made for saturation coverage.

Then, ask students to think of other similar cases where the press and media have been responsible for changing our views of a public figure, either for better or worse. Suggest some names to research on the Internet if students are unsure (for example, Michael Barrymore, Cheryl Cole, Jonathan Ross and Russell Brand, David Blunkett, Coleen Rooney).

Ask students, in pairs, to read through Resource 4.2 on British news values, comparing the way the two news stories have been reported. They should then discuss in pairs the questions that follow, aiming to find answers on which they both agree.

Plenary:

As a class discuss your conclusions to the questions on Resource 4.2. Is their a general consensus among students?

Extension activity:

Both Kate and Gerry McCann and Jade Goody had previously enjoyed a positive relationship with the press. However, the press turned on them eventually and the public changed their opinions of these people with very little additional evidence.

Think of cases where the media have either built someone up from nothing to stardom, or done the opposite and destroyed their careers.

Lesson Two: Politics and the media

Learning objectives:

- To identify the qualities we look for in a leader
- To understand that different media outlets can support a particular political party or position
- To recognize the ways a politician or political party can use the media to their advantage.

Resources: 4.3, 4.4, 4.5, 4.6

Starter:

Use a beanbag or something soft, and ask the whole class to stand up, preferably in a circle. Explain that when the beanbag is thrown to you, you must call out a quality that you think should be important in a good politician or leader. You must say the word before you catch the beanbag. The words should basically be a list of all the ideal traits we look for in good leaders. For example, trust, good communication, honesty, friendliness.

Main activity:

The media recognizes that it plays a powerful role in shaping or even altering people's opinions. Politicians often face a very difficult task of overcoming negative representation in the media.

Ask students to read through the report on Tony Blair's first day as prime minister on Resource 4.3, thinking about what overall impression of the Prime Minister it intends to convey, underlining words and phrases that help shape their opinions. They then need to read through the report of Gordon Brown's first day (also on Resource 4.3), before comparing the words used to describe each leader using Resource 4.4. Both articles are about the first day of a new prime minister, but the tone is completely different.

When they have finished the task, facilitate a class discussion on how the media shape our opinions of politicians' personalities.

Explain to the class that the next activity will be about looking at the relationship between politicians and the media.

Politicians spend a great deal of time and energy trying to persuade newspaper editors to support them and their political parties as they recognize how important the media is in influencing the public. Increasingly, politicians will prioritize issues that are in the headlines, as they know they will get more media coverage that way. For example:

- Youth crime
- Immigration
- Teenage pregnancy
- Celebrity stories.

Politicians often feel that they have to be *seen* to be 'talking tough' on issues that are high on the media agenda. The problem is that this can lead to the media not politicians deciding which stories/issues deserve the most attention.

Split the class into four groups and ask each group to elect one person as the editor of their paper and the rest are the journalists that make up the editorial team. Provide the editor of each team with a copy of Resource 4.5 and ask them to share the information and the task with the rest of their group. The group must discuss the course of action the newspaper editor should take in the face of a corrupt leader. The group must then write a front page for *The Evening Sun* newspaper based on their decision. They should present their front page to the rest of the class and explain what decisions were taken as a group and what arguments there may have been during the process.

Next, working in groups of two or three, students must read through and discuss Resource 4.6, thinking about what kinds of stories would support each point of the politician's manifesto. Students need to consider what type of story will support his aims, and how these stories can be conveyed without the public realizing the paper is supporting a particular political angle.

Plenary:
Ask each group to give a short presentation outlining their media campaign.

Extension activity:
Allocate each of the stories from the campaign to a group member. Write the newspaper stories for the media campaign.

Lesson Three: Endorsement

Learning objectives:

- To understand that endorsement of an advertising campaign by a famous personality can influence its outcome
- To recognize the different audiences that products or campaigns are marketed towards
- To identify the personal qualities associated with famous personalities and how these might appeal to an audience.

Resources: 4.7, 4.8, 4.9

Starter:
Ask students to read through the examples of celebrity fronted campaigns on Resource 4.7 and to list three reasons celebrities might want to be involved with a campaign.

Main activity:
Read through Resource 4.8 and, if possible, show students an example of the advertising campaign. These can be viewed via the M&C Saatchi website: www.mcsaatchi.com/work_detail.php?workid=112, or via YouTube™ (www.youtube.com). Ask students to script a one-minute advert featuring Prince Charles – an unlikely policeman – thinking about what he would say. Ask some students to act out their adverts.

Use Resource 4.9 for the next activity. This task works best if you are in a setting where students have access to computers for Internet research. Ask students, in pairs, to answer question one to work through the list of eight celebrities. They need to research their personalities and then decide on the ideal products for them to advertise, as well as devise a slogan appropriate to both them *and* the product.

Plenary:
Discuss as a class the slogans students have come up with for each celebrity. Can students identify any common themes? Which do they think are particularly effective?

Extension activity:
Students could answer question two on the resource to choose one of their celebrity/product pairings and design a billboard advertisement.

Lesson Four: Campaign backing

Learning objectives:

- To identify the target audience for a given campaign or product
- To identify a suitable personality to front a campaign and the most suitable media to reach the target audience.

Resources: 4.10, 4.11, 4.12

Starter:
As the class walk into the lesson, hand each of them the used packaging from a well-known product. These should be things that are easily obtainable. Examples include:

- Chocolate bar wrapper
- Cereal box
- Supermarket voucher
- Egg carton

Explain to students that they have three minutes to think of who would be the ideal person to front an advertisement for their product and why, and to think of an appropriate slogan for the advert.

Each member of the class must then hold up their 'product' and explain who they chose to front the campaign and why they would be appropriate.

Main activity:
Before the lesson, gather as many examples of charity advertisements featuring celebrity endorsements as possible. Contacting charities directly and asking them to send examples of such campaigns is a good way to get a sizeable number. The Internet is also a good resource for this and will allow you to collate famous historical examples for the class to view. Other good places to look include the library, the town hall, the Citizens Advice Bureau or just collect them as they arrive through your front door!

Split the class into five groups and give each group a cause. For example:

1. Natural beauty
2. Cancer care
3. Encouraging young people to vote
4. Better care for the elderly
5. Anti-obesity

In their groups, using Resource 4.10, students must discuss their campaign and decide on the best celebrity to front their cause, ensuring they take their target audience into account. They must also come up with a slogan, and decide on which method of advertising their campaign will use, before completing the table on Resource 4.11.

Halfway through this exercise, you might decide to share Resource 4.12 to enable them to re-evaluate their choices.

Plenary:
Ask each group to present their work on their table. Spend the last five to ten minutes of the lesson with each group inviting the rest of the class over to view their work and hear about how the decisions were made.

Extension/Assessment activity:
Using their chosen method, ask students to script an advert, thinking about the words they would use, and where and when the advert would be broadcast/posted.

Resource 4.1: Saturation coverage

The media often set the agenda for what we talk about in society. If all the newspapers cover the same stories and this is reflected on the television, on the radio and on the Internet, then issues can become blown up out of proportion. Also, people may take their opinion from what they read in newspapers rather than forming their own opinions. Here are two stories that received a large amount of coverage.

Case study one: Disappearance of Madeleine McCann

Madeleine McCann disappeared on the evening of Thursday 3 May 2007 while on holiday with her parents and twin siblings in the Algarve region of Portugal. The British girl went missing from an apartment, in the central area of the resort of Praia da Luz, a few days before her fourth birthday. Madeleine's parents, Kate and Gerry McCann, have said that they left the children unsupervised in a ground floor bedroom while they ate at a restaurant about 100 yards away but checked on them at regular intervals.

The disappearance and its aftermath were notable for the sheer amount of media coverage. Originally the media were involved because Madeleine's parents wanted to publicize their case and appeal for help. However, many felt this backfired when the media turned against Maddie's parents and were suspicious of the family and their role in their daughter's disappearance. The newspapers covered this story heavily over the summer of 2007.

Various newspapers have since had to pay damages for printing inaccurate information. Express Newspapers paid Kate and Gerry McCann £550,000 in damages in March 2008, after alleging that the couple were responsible for the death of their daughter in a series of articles.

Case study two: *Celebrity Big Brother* racism row

In 2007 the Channel 4 reality television series *Celebrity Big Brother* was at the centre of a racism row. Three white female contestants were accused of displaying racist behaviour towards Shilpa Shetty, an Indian Bollywood actress. The contestants accused of racism included Jade Goody, a contestant in the third series of *Big Brother*. Goody had received a huge amount of media coverage both good and bad following her rise to fame. She become a magazine and newspaper regular, released successful books and DVDs and appeared on a number of other reality television shows.

The contestants' racist remarks were shown on air, resulting in record numbers of complaints from the public. The media coverage focused on Jade Goody and Shilpa Shetty as being at the centre of the row. The complaints were covered by national and international media, leading to both the UK and Indian governments becoming involved.

During the investigation into the allegations of racism, the Carphone Warehouse cancelled their sponsorship deal with Endemol, the programme's producer. The accused contestants, including Jade Goody and Danielle Lloyd, also lost personal sponsorship deals.

After the show, Jade Goody accepted that her comments were racist and apologized for them. Shilpa Shetty later told the media that she forgave Jade.

As a consequence of the controversy caused by the racism row, the 2008 series of *Celebrity Big Brother* was cancelled.

Jade Goody was diagnosed with cervical cancer in August 2008. It was confirmed in February 2009 that her illness was terminal. She fought a high-profile battle with the disease and died in March 2009.

---

1. What are the ingredients in these stories that meant the British newspapers provided 'saturation coverage' (front page stories every day) for several weeks?

Resource 4.2: British news values

The British media tends to focus on news stories that they feel are of particular interest to Britons. This can lead to similar news stories from different countries being given an unequal amount of attention. Similarly, there is sometimes criticism that the British media focuses predominantly on the news stories of people who are culturally similar to the British, such as, Australians or Americans. For example, most people on Earth could name the President of America, but how many know the name of the current Chinese leader is President Hu Jintao? He is arguably as important to the world and its future.

Saturday 5 May 2007
Kenyan plane crashes in Cameroon

A Kenya Airways plane with 114 people on board has reportedly crashed in southern Cameroon.

The flight, which originated in Ivory Coast, was reported missing on Saturday after it failed to arrive in Kenya.

People from at least 23 different nationalities were on board, including five Britons, the airline said.

Kenya's national carrier has a good safety record. However, 169 people died when one of its planes crashed in 2000.

(available at http://news.bbc.co.uk/1/hi/world/africa/6627485.stm)

Friday 16 January 2009
Miracle on the Hudson: 155 survive crash as jet hits river in New York

The pilot of a US Airways jet managed to avoid disaster and save the lives of all 155 people on board his stricken plane when he ditched into the icy waters of the Hudson River moments after taking off from New York's LaGuardia airport.

The extraordinary escape was immediately dubbed the miracle on the Hudson, and hailed as a testimony to the ability of New York to cope with disaster in the wake of 9/11. Flight 1549 was carrying 148 passengers, including a baby, five crew and two pilots, and all of them escaped.

The captain, named last night as Chesley Sullenberger, has 29 years' experience with commercial airlines and is a former US airforce fighter pilot.

With both his twin engines in trouble, one apparently on fire, and with the nearest airport out of range, he calmly brought the plane to land on the river on the west side of Manhattan.

A mere 30 to 45 seconds after take-off there was a bang and the aircraft shook, believed to have been caused by it striking a flock of geese.

The pilot reported to air traffic control that he was experiencing engine problems and requested to return to ground. The nearest identified airport was in New Jersey, but when it became clear he could not make it, the pilot prepared for a crash landing on the Hudson. "Brace yourself for impact," he told the passengers.

Seconds later the plane struck the Hudson, on a line with 48th Street in midtown Manhattan, turning a stretch of waterway normally populated by tourists enjoying a waterside view of the skyscrapers into an astonishing fight for survival.

Eyewitnesses reported seeing a splash and the plane coming to an immediate stop; it looked so controlled that some witnesses mistook it for the landing of a seaplane.

The survival of all on board appears to have been thanks to a combination of the plane remaining intact on impact and almost immediate assistance from at least seven water taxis and tugs which swarmed around the jet.

(available at www.guardian.co.uk/world/2009/jan/16/us-airways-plane-crash-lands-on-hudson)

In pairs, discuss the following questions and find answers you can agree on:

1. Which of the plane crash stories is the most important and why?
2. Why does the British media report stories concerning the USA in so much more detail?
3. Do the media have a responsibility to report all news stories equally?

Article 1

We are a nation reborn

Andrew Rawnsley, The Observer, Saturday 3 May 1997

On Friday morning Britain woke up a different country. It may be a trick of the light, but it feels like a younger country ... When Tony Blair's party last won an election he was still the lead singer in a college rock group; when it last had a working majority he was still in short trousers; when it last had a landslide he was not even a twinkle in his father's eye. The average age of the Cabinet has dropped by about 10 years. In spirit they are 20 years fresher than the faces they replace ... Labour offers at least the illusion of marking a new beginning, and is offered the opportunity to make it a reality ... The sound of young children will echo around the house of power for the first time [since 1916]. We have [now] a Prime Minister who buys his leisure shirts from Gap. Macaroni cheese is no longer the dish of choice in Downing Street. It is more likely to be tortellini pesto.

[This] is a Prime Minister who prefers to spend his time with young footballers. After six and a half years under a leader whose vision was of a Britain wearing a cardigan and slumbering over a warm beer ... we now have a Prime Minister who styles himself a 'modern man'. Tony Blair will be the first Prime Minister to send his children to state schools ...

It is a long, long time since we had a Prime Minister who could not only speak French, but speak it with sufficient fluency not to embarrass us or himself in front of the French.

That a revolution has begun no one can surely doubt.

Article 2

Will Gordon Brown really change the face of British politics?

Nicholas Watt, Political Editor, The Observer, Sunday 1 July 2007

Tapping the microphone in the manner of a nervous compere, ... Brown walked slowly up to the entrance of No. 10.

No hand-picked crowds waving union flags lined the street. Only the media were on hand to hear Brown's brief statement, [very different to] Blair's first appearance before ecstatic crowds on 2 May 1997. Flanked by his wife Sarah, Brown spoke of how his schooling in Kirkcaldy, Fife, had inspired him. 'On this day I remember words that have stayed with me since my childhood and which matter a great deal to me today: my school motto, "I will try my utmost". This is my promise to all of the people of Britain,' he said.

With that, the Browns turned and walked slowly into Downing Street.

Brown will be up, as ever, in the early hours of this morning. As his two young sons noisily wake up the rest of the household, Brown will slip out of his bedroom and into his study where he will sit down at his computer to prepare for his first encounter as Prime Minister.

'So far so good,' one departing cabinet minister said of Brown's debut. 'Let's just see what happens when the going gets tough.'

Resource 4.4: Political agendas
in the media II

1. Read through Article 1 on Resource 4.3 twice. It was published two days after Tony Blair took office in May 2007. What impression do you reach of the new Prime Minster? Underline any words or phrases that you think make the Prime Minister a good choice for the country, and write them in the box below.

2. After reading Article 1, try and sum up in five words what impression the journalist is giving of Tony Blair in his first two days in office.

3. Read through Article 2 on Resource 4.3 twice. What impression do you gain of Gordon Brown? Underline any words and phrases that help to shape your opinion, and write them in the box below.

4. After reading Article 2, try to sum up in five words what impression the journalist is giving of Gordon Brown.

5. Compare the five words you chose to describe Tony Blair and the five words you chose to describe Gordon Brown. What are the main differences in the ways the two men's actions are described?

Resource 4.5: The moral media

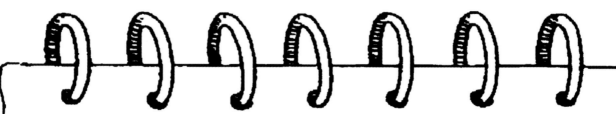

You are a newspaper editor in a small developing country. Your country was governed for 25 years by the same man and things were good. He led the people well and he did his best to ensure that the country was stable and that people were happy.

He died a year ago and his nephew is now the leader of the country. He was not elected by the people and is unpopular, aggressive and violent. He drinks heavily and there is evidence that he also uses illegal drugs often. He has turned a peaceful and successful nation into one filled with paranoia, hunger and fear. Those who complain about the leader are taken away by the army in big grey vans late at night. They never return.

You write for one of the country's newspapers, *The Evening Sun*, and your job is to tell the truth and write about the important issues in your country. You have countless stories, photos and other evidence of incidents of rape, violence and murder committed by soldiers in the leader's name.

Tomorrow marks the first anniversary of your leader taking power in your country. It is an ideal date to publish an article about your leader. Will you run a front-page story exposing the violence, murder, corruption, drinking and drug-taking of your leader and his army?

Decide what you are going to report on the front page of your newspaper for the next day.

Consider the following points:

- The safety of your families, the rest of the staff at the newspaper and maybe some members of the public caught reading the article.
- You personally have enough money to leave the country and start a new life in a different country. However, none of your friends or colleagues at the newspaper can afford to leave the country.
- You love your country. Your family has lived there for many generations and it is a place of great natural beauty.
- Will anything change if you publish the story?
- The rest of world is taking no interest in the troubles of your nation. Your country is poor, it has no natural resources such as oil, and you feel that the people of your country are being left to suffer their fate whilst the world turns its back and closes its eyes.

Write the front-page story for tomorrow's edition of *The Evening Sun*.

Resource 4.6: The political media

You are a young-ish, passionate and committed politician in a small town in the south of England and you are determined to make a difference in your local area. The same group of politicians has been running the town for 37 years and you are sure that what is needed are some new ideas and different thinking. You have loads of new ideas for the area and you have written your own manifesto, highlighting your plans for the town:

- ♣ All young people to be kept off the streets by new 8.30pm curfew
- ♣ No large vehicles (people carriers or 4x4 cars) to be driven in the centre of town
- ♣ All members of the community must speak, understand or be in the process of learning English
- ♣ No alcohol to be consumed on the streets
- ♣ No mobile phone conversations allowed on any public transport
- ♣ Free football tickets for the local team for children under 12 years old
- ♣ In order to claim their benefits, the long-term unemployed must work cleaning the town.

You have just one year until the next important council elections.

Your best friend is the editor of the local free newspaper that goes into every home in the town. He has agreed to help you by running news stories that will benefit your campaign.

You need to plan a news story for each manifesto point. This is an organized media campaign so you need to look over the year January–January and decide when you should run each story to benefit the manifesto point to maximum effect. Decide which are the most powerful manifesto points and leave those stories until nearer the election on 10 January.

Each story should be designed to support your manifesto, but without the public realizing that it is supporting a particular political angle.

You have only 12 months and seven news stories to write and you need to get the stories and timing just right in order to get yourselves elected by the public on 10 January. You have to make your ideas seem like the common-sense choice for the town.

1. Make a plan for each news story. Make notes on:
   - the key points for each story
   - why it supports your manifesto
   - when you will run the story and why.

2. Write your newspaper articles for your media campaign.

Resource 4.7: Celebrity campaigns

Campaigns often gain a lot of publicity if they are endorsed or publicly supported by a celebrity. Newspapers and the media in general are much more likely to offer publicity to a cause if it has a famous face fronting the campaign. The following campaigns have become synonymous with certain high-profile celebrities.

Child poverty in Africa – Bono

"Africa is bursting into flames while we stand around with watering cans".

Pro-gun lobby (USA) – Charlton Heston

"I intend to dedicate my remaining time as president of the NRA (National Rifle Association) to ensure that the Second Amendment is safe from Al Gore and all those who threaten it."

The second amendment is part of the Constitution of the USA which says every person should have the right to keep and bear arms; to own a gun to defend themselves.

Anti-Heathrow expansion – Emma Thompson

"I don't understand how any government remotely serious about committing to reversing climate change can even consider these ridiculous plans. It's laughably hypocritical."

Healthy school meals – Jamie Oliver

"Many kids can tell you about drugs but do not know what celery or courgettes taste like."

Think of three reasons why a celebrity would want to get involved in endorsing a campaign.

1. _____

2. _____

3. _____

Citizenship through informed and responsible action © Folens (copiable page)

Resource 4.8: 'Could You? Police' campaign

In 2000, the government launched the first national police recruitment campaign. After a decline in the numbers of police officers and the number of applicants with the right attitude and qualifications, the Home Office launched an advertising campaign to recruit new officers. The campaign also came in the wake of the Macpherson report into the murder of Stephen Lawrence, which recommended the increased recruitment of officers from minority ethnic groups. The government worked with the famous advertising company M&C Saatchi to produce a series of high-profile television advertisements.

The adverts featured prominent British celebrities from a range of backgrounds, including:

- Simon Weston – Falklands War veteran
- John Barnes – black British footballer, former England International
- Joan Bakewell – broadcaster, journalist and feminist
- Patsy Palmer – actor, starred in *EastEnders*
- Lennox Lewis – black British boxer, former Heavyweight World Champion
- Chris Bisson – British Asian actor, starred in *Coronation Street* and films such as *East is East*

Each celebrity talked about the situations they might find themselves in as police officers, such as telling a father about the death of his wife and child or confronting football hooligans. One advert featured Falklands hero Simon Weston, former Welsh Guard who was badly burnt when the Argentinean Air Force bombed his landing ship. He says: "People say I'm brave but going round to someone's house, people I've never met before, to tell a man that his wife and child have been killed in a car crash … I'm not sure I could do that."

All the adverts featured a celebrity considering one aspect of the job of a police officer and saying they would struggle to cope with the challenges they face. They conclude "I could not do it. Could you?"

The campaign sent out the message that it takes a talented individual to become a police officer and asked viewers to put themselves in that position and consider whether they could do it. It aimed to demonstrate the challenges the police face and to raise the status of the service in the eyes of the public.

1. The 'Could You? Police' adverts rely on using well-known British figures from backgrounds not associated with the police force. Using the website www.policecouldyou.co.uk to help you find out about the role of a police officer, script a one-minute 'Could You? Police' advert. Prince Charles is not from a police background; use Prince Charles as the celebrity in your advert and imagine what he could say to convince people to join the police.

_____

_____

_____

_____

_____

_____

_____

Resource 4.9: Finding the right public face

When choosing a celebrity to be the public face of your product or cause, you need to consider the public personality of a celebrity and then match it to an appropriate product.

Leona Lewis: *X Factor* winner

Leona Lewis > natural talent > multicultural > modesty > popular with women > shyness > public support > girl next door appeal ...

The ideal product for Leona would be something for ordinary/everyday women to own that would enhance their natural talent/beauty. Leona's type of fame or beauty is built around the fact that it is achievable for everybody. It should be reasonably priced as her main fan base is not particularly wealthy.

Ideal product: Hair straighteners

Slogan: "Unlock YOUR star potential."

José Mourinho: European football manager

José Mourinho > European > uncompromising > arrogant > determined > charismatic > inspiring > winner > sex symbol > envied by men ...

The ideal product for José to advertise would be one for confident men who are aware of their own attractiveness. The product should also have some 'snob' value and should not be too cheap, definitely not affordable for everybody. It should be a product that women like and one that men want to own as a way to improve their image and set them apart from the rest.

Ideal product: European prestige car

Slogan: "Live, as you were born to live."

1. Research the following eight celebrities and find out about their public personalities and what values they could represent in a product.

   - Andy Murray – tennis player
   - Jeremy Kyle – talkshow host
   - Rebecca Adlington – swimmer and double Olympic gold medallist 2008
   - Prince Harry – third in line to the throne
   - Pam St. Clement – Pat Butcher from *EastEnders*
   - Matt LeBlanc – Joey from *Friends*
   - Mutya Buena – singer, ex-Sugababe
   - Daniel Radcliffe – *Harry Potter* actor

   Choose a product for each of them to advertise, and write a slogan appropriate to both them *and* the product.

2. Choose your favourite celebrity and product pairing and create a professional-looking A4 version of a billboard advert. Remember the end product MUST feature:

   - a picture of the celebrity
   - a picture of the product
   - the campaign slogan.

Resource 4.10: Our campaign 1

You have been given a cause and are going to devise a compaign to promote it.

1. Discuss the aims of your campaign, bearing in mind the message you want to send out about your cause and who your target audience will be.
2. Decide on the most appropriate form of media to use to get your message across.
3. Choose a high-profile person to front the campaign.
4. Write a new slogan for the campaign.

Make notes in the box below before completing Resource 4.11.

Remember!
Not *all* methods of advertising are suitable for *all* target audiences. Pop-up Internet adverts may work well with teenage audiences, but are less likely to be very effective with older people. Remember to consider all the different types of media advertising that are available:

- newspapers/television/magazines
- radio
- Internet
- leaflets
- direct advertising (people approaching you on the streets)
- large billboard advertising
- bus shelters and/or bus tickets
- cinema

Remember!
Don't make the advertising campaign so sensible that it becomes too predictable and boring. Getting Gok Wan or Trinny and Susannah to front a campaign about natural beauty is just too simple, as they are already strongly identified with these issues. So, don't always go for the obvious choice of celebrity. Do some research about the personal life, the achievements or even the failures of your chosen public figure to make sure they are appropriate.

Resource 4.11: Our campaign 2

After discussing your campaign, complete the table below:

Product/cause	
Main target audience	
Slogan	
Method of advertising	
Chosen celebrity	

Citizenship through informed and responsible action   © Folens (copiable page)

Resource 4.12: A change of plan!

Is there a problem with starting a campaign driven by a celebrity and then realizing that something in their personal lives makes them an unsuitable choice?

An example of this was Fern Britton who fronted the campaign for Ryvita (a brand of healthy snacks) after losing a remarkable amount of weight in a short period of time. She inspired thousands of women who then felt let down when it was revealed that a medical procedure was the real reason behind her dramatic weight loss.

Fern Britton admits real reason for weight loss

TV presenter Fern Britton has admitted that she underwent stomach surgery in order to lose weight.

Britton, co-host of *This Morning* on ITV had previously claimed her weight loss had been due to eating a healthy diet and taking regular exercise, such as cycling and walking the family dog.

The presenter, who has lost three stone over the last two years and dropped from a size 22 to a size 16, has now admitted having a gastric band. The procedure involves surgically implanting a band to physically limit the size of the stomach.

This reduces the amount of food that can be eaten.

Britton made a statement regarding her weight loss: "As I know, many people are interested in my weight loss of the past two years. As interest is so high I'm making public, as a personal choice, that I had a gastric band operation two years ago."

She went on to say that she was "very pleased with the results", but did say that the decision to have the surgery had been a purely personal one and that she would not wish to influence others to have the same procedure.

Theme five
Taking action

In this final theme of the book, students are required to take all that they have learnt in the previous themes and take ownership of a campaign to achieve change. This section has been written based on learning drawn from RECLAIM, an active Citizenship project coordinated by the authors and delivered by Urbis in Manchester.

RECLAIM is an award-winning leadership and mentoring project that helps young people take action in their communities. The project begins with a four-day conference which sees the young people meeting inspirational speakers, devising a youth manifesto and working to create positive change.

RECLAIM began working with a group of 13–14 year olds in 2007 in response to the worrying levels of youth crime in South Manchester, centring on Moss Side, an area blighted in recent years by a series of high-profile killings. Directed by the agenda of its young members, RECLAIM has since empowered some of the most disadvantaged young people to engage directly with the decision-makers influencing their lives. By promoting leadership and encouraging dialogue with the police, council and media, those who are often marginalized have been helped to realize their voice.

Further information can be found at: www.reclaimproject.org.uk

In this theme, the students will have to be highly motivated and organized. The teacher role becomes one of facilitating the groups and overseeing the progress made, and ensuring that all students are engaged in their work.

In the project groups there are a variety of different roles available to allow the students to operate confidently and to work semi-independently. The groups should be well chosen to ensure that each contains a varied selection of students from a range of attainment levels. The key to success with this theme is to allow enough time for planning and preparation and then for a full evaluation at the end. These are often the weakest areas for students. Stress the importance of them having a strategic overview of the project and therefore some control over its direction.

Encourage the groups to make contact with organizations that can aid them in their project and also to use digital technology to maximize the impact of their work, for example setting up Facebook groups and blogging about their progress.

Finally, encourage students to use their work to create displays as part of the evaluation so they can see the results of their hard work and dedication whenever they enter the classroom!

Further resources on taking action can be found at the links below:

- www.getglobal.org.uk: Get Global, a skills-based approach to facilitating and assessing active global Citizenship.
- www.studentvoice.co.uk/campaignforchange: English Secondary Students' Association's Campaign for Change
- http://handbook.battlefront.co.uk: Battlefront's Campaigner's Handbook
- www.bl.uk/learning/histcitizen/index.html: The British Library's website for History and Citizenship

Theme aims:

- To give students the opportunity to apply active Citizenship processes to a campaign of their choice.
- To evaluate the effectiveness of their action.
- To work independently towards established aims and objectives.

Lesson One: Identifying your target

Learning objectives:

- To identify roles for all group members, considering the personal qualities that qualify them for the role
- To identify a campaign and define its aims
- To decide on a group name and devise a tagline, manifesto and mantra.

Resources: 5.1, 5.2, 5.3

Starter:

Introduce the class to the project that will take them through the next six lessons. Explain that this will be an opportunity for them to put all they have learnt so far into practice. Split the class into groups of 6–8 students. In their groups, students will need to come up with an idea to create change on an issue *they* think is important. This lesson will be spent working out a strategy to put their ideas into practice.

Remind students that they will need to decide now how they will make decisions within their group – will one person be a leader who has the final say or will they vote democratically?

Groups now need to allocate roles to each member (Resource 5.1) and work through the tasks to plan their project (Resources 5.2 and 5.3).

Lessons Two to Four: Using your voice

Learning objectives:

- To gain practice in self-directed research and project planning
- To use a variety of sources to research a chosen subject, to evaluate these sources and use information to inform action
- To persuade others of a point view and gain support, including from people with influence in the chosen issue
- To produce visual and textual materials to promote the project.

Main activity:

Groups to continue self-directed project planning. Students should be responsible for arranging their own meetings and self-directed group tasks.

Lesson Five: Action in action

Learning objectives:

- To deliver an active Citizenship event, project or campaign
- To explain the project and persuade others to support its aims
- To record and document activities undertaken and gather feedback from the group and others.

Main activity:

Groups carry out their Citizenship project, campaign or event.

Lesson Six: Evaluating your results

Learning objectives:

- To evaluate the success of the project and to identify areas that could have been improved
- To utilize presentation skills to describe the project, and its strengths and weaknesses, to others.

Resource: 5.4

Plenary:

Each group gives a presentation about their project, including how they evaluated their success (Resource 5.4). Make sure students are given a copy of the resource well in advance in order to prepare for the presentation.

Resource 5.1: Role allocation

In your groups, you will need to decide on roles for each person, allocating someone to each of the following posts. When deciding, think about the personal qualities of each group member, their skills and talents, and what would make them good at the job.

Spokesperson: You will front the campaign, make speeches and presentations and talk to the media. You'll also inspire and motivate other members of the group.

Essential qualities: confidence, charisma, good at public speaking.

Researcher: You will research the issue, making sure to find out all the important arguments, facts and figures that will make your project a success. You will need to gather lots of information, and ensure the rest of the group is aware of the important bits!

Essential qualities: good at finding things out, using the Internet and other sources to gather information.

Campaigner: You will ensure that your group's message is communicated to the people with influence. You might write letters to the people with power, gather petitions or hand out leaflets to the public.

Essential qualities: good communication skills, good at prioritizing, perseverance!

Artist: You will be responsible for designing and producing artwork for the project, ensuring the group's message is conveyed through your visuals. This could include leaflets, posters, placards, T-shirts or web pages.

Essential qualities: creativity, visual awareness, able to produce high-quality finished materials such as posters.

Fundraiser: You will encourage people to donate money or resources to your cause. This might mean enlisting people to sponsor you or speaking to local businesses to see if they can donate anything.

Essential qualities: good communicator, persuasiveness, perseverance.

Public relations: You will find opportunities to publicize your project, to make sure as many people as possible know about it. This might mean contacting local newspapers or broadcasters, using social networking sites, finding places to display posters or sending out invitations.

Essential qualities: good communication skills, initiative, persuasiveness.

Coordinator: You will oversee the activities of the rest of the group and make sure each member is meeting their targets. You'll also be responsible for arranging things like venues, extra meetings for your group and so on. You will ensure the group's message is consistent and that all tasks are achieved on time.

Essential qualities: good organization, timekeeping, able to motivate others.

Resource 5.2: Planning your project

1. Decide on your issue. It might help to draw a mindmap so the ideas of all group members get put down on paper. You may want to think about:

   - Topics you've already covered so far in your Citizenship classes that you may have found interesting.
   - Something you'd like to change in your school or local area.
   - Global or national issues you think more people should be aware of.

2. Work out who will be your target audience. Who has the most power to create change on your chosen topic and how can you influence them?

Remember!

Play to your strengths. If your group has particular skills such as web design or film-making, use them!

Be realistic. Don't attempt to make a film if no one in your group knows how to and you don't have the resources or equipment to do it.

Sometimes simple ideas are the most effective!

3. Decide what action you will take to create change. You might decide to organize an event to raise awareness, start a letter-writing campaign, hold a fundraising event or lobby your local council about your issue. Think carefully about what you want to achieve, and then work out the best way to do it.

4. Decide on three aims that you would like to achieve by the end of your project. They need to be realistic and achievable within the amount of time you have.

   a. _____

   b. _____

   c. _____

   These could be goals like: 'Raise £50 for a local elderly care home'. Or 'Send a petition to stop deforestation of the Amazon rainforest with at least 200 signatures to our local MP'.

   Be ambitious, but don't set your sights too high! It would be unrealistic to aim to completely eradicate animal testing or to raise £1 million with your project, for example.

5. At the end of your project, you will use your aims to judge whether your project was a success or not – did your project meet all of its aims? You will also be expected to give a presentation to your class, so as you plan and carry out your project remember to:

   - Keep records of your event so you can demonstrate what you did later on
   - Take photos
   - Save copies of any letters you have sent or received
   - Count how many people you spoke to or came to your event
   - Record the amount of money you raised.

   You might also want to keep a book so people can write feedback or messages of support.

Resource 5.3: Motivating the group

1. Decide on a group name (but don't spend all your time on this!) and come up with a manifesto for your project that states a set of shared rules/ideas to guide your group.

MANIFESTO

Group name:

1. _____

2. _____

3. _____

4. _____

5. _____

6. _____

7. _____

8. _____

---

2. Create a tagline for your campaign:

---

3. Create a group mantra to help you stay focused and achieve your aims:

Resource 5.4: Presenting your project

You will give a group presentation, around 15–20 minutes long, about your project to the rest of the class.

In your presentation you need to:

- Give a clear introduction, stating the aims your project set out to achieve.
- Give a description of your project activities. What did you do to achieve your aims and why?
- Share your mantra, manifesto and campaign tagline.
- Evaluate your results. This is an important element of any active Citizenship project. It helps to tell you and others if you managed to achieve your goals, and identifies areas you could improve on.
- Give a clear conclusion to finish your presentation, stating whether your project was a success or not, based on your evaluation.

As you are evaluating your project, ask yourself the following important questions. Try to cover them all and provide your answers in your presentation.

1. What worked particularly well?

_____

_____

2. What could have been done better?

_____

_____

3. What do other people think? Did you collect any feedback?

_____

_____

4. Did you achieve the three aims you set out at the start of the project?

_____

_____

5. How can you prove your project was a success? Evidence you could collect to show others what you achieved might include:

- photos taken at your event
- letters you wrote or received
- posters you designed
- numbers of people who attended your event or signed your petition
- the amount of money you raised.

Citizenship through informed and responsible action © Folens (copiable page)